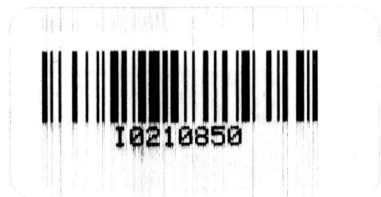

Names for Jesus

Names for Jesus

Reflections for Advent and Christmas

Mark G. Boyer

WIPF & STOCK · Eugene, Oregon

NAMES FOR JESUS
Reflections for Advent and Christmas

Copyright © 2017 Mark G. Boyer. All rights reserved. Except for brief
quotations in critical publications or reviews, no part of this book may
be reproduced in any manner without prior written permission from the
publisher. Write: Permissions, Wipf and Stock Publishers, 199 W. 8th Ave.,
Suite 3, Eugene, OR 97401.

Wipf & Stock
An Imprint of Wipf and Stock Publishers
199 W. 8th Ave., Suite 3
Eugene, OR 97401

www.wipfandstock.com

PAPERBACK ISBN: 978-1-5326-3261-7
HARDCOVER ISBN: 978-1-5326-3263-1
EBOOK ISBN: 978-1-5326-3262-4

The Scripture quotations contained herein are from the New Revised
Standard Version Bible, copyright © 1989 by the Division of Christian
Education of the National Council of the Churches of Christ in the
U.S.A., and are used by permission. All rights reserved.

Manufactured in the U.S.A.

Dedicated to
friend and fellow traveler
Corbin S. Cole

"... [A]t the name of Jesus
every knee should bend,
in heaven and on earth and under the earth,
and every tongue should confess
that Jesus Christ is Lord,
to the glory of God the Father."

—Phil 2:10–11

Contents

Abbreviations

CB (NT)	**Christian Bible (New Testament)**
Acts	Acts of the Apostles
Col	Letter to the Colossians
1 Cor	First Letter of Paul to the Corinthians
2 Cor	Second Letter of Paul to the Corinthians
Eph	Letter to the Ephesians
Gal	Letter of Paul to the Galatians
Heb	Letter to the Hebrews
John	John's Gospel
1 John	First Letter of John
Luke	Luke's Gospel
Mark	Mark's Gospel
Matt	Matthew's Gospel
1 Pet	First Letter of Peter
2 Pet	Second Letter of Peter
Phil	Letter of Paul to the Philippians
Rev	Book of Revelation
Rom	Letter of Paul to the Romans
1 Thess	First Letter of Paul to the Thessalonians
1 Tim	First Letter to Timothy
2 Tim	Second Letter to Timothy

HB (OT)   Hebrew Bible (Old Testament)

Dan	Daniel
Deut	Deuteronomy
Exod	Exodus
Ezek	Ezekiel
Gen	Genesis
Hos	Hosea
Isa	Isaiah
Jer	Jeremiah
Mal	Malachi
Mic	Micah
Num	Numbers
Prov	Proverbs
Ps	Psalm

OT (A)   Old Testament (Apocrypha)

2 Macc	Second Book of Maccabees
Sir	Sirach (Ecclesiasticus)

The Bible

The Bible is divided into two parts: The Hebrew Bible (Old Testament) and the Christian Bible (New Testament). The Hebrew Bible consists of thirty-nine named books accepted by Jews and Protestants as Holy Scripture. The Old Testament also contains those thirty-nine books plus seven to fifteen more named books or parts of books called the Apocrypha or the Deuterocanonical Books; the Old Testament is accepted by Catholics and several other Christian denominations as Holy Scripture. The Christian Bible, consisting of twenty-seven named books, is also called the New Testament; it is accepted by Christians as Holy Scripture. Thus, in this work:

- Hebrew Bible (Old Testament), abbreviated HB (OT), indicates that a book is found both in the Hebrew Bible and the Old Testament;

- Old Testament (Apocrypha), abbreviated OT (A), indicates that a book is found only in the Old Testament Apocrypha and not in the Hebrew Bible;

- and Christian Bible (New Testament), abbreviated CB (NT), indicates that a book is found only in the Christian Bible or New Testament.

Unless otherwise noted, the *New Revised Standard Version* (NRSV) Bible is used throughout this work. In notating biblical texts, the first number refers to the chapter in the book, and the second number refers to the verse within the chapter. Thus, HB (OT) Isa 7:11 means that the quotation comes from Isaiah, chapter 7, verse 11. OT (A) Sirach 39:30 means that the quotation comes from Sirach, chapter 39, verse 30. CB (NT) Mark 6:2 means that the quotation comes from Mark's Gospel, chapter 6, verse 2.

Introduction

Title

This book is titled *Names for Jesus*. Throughout the Christian Bible (New Testament), the various authors of the books contained therein use a variety of names for Jesus. However, there are also names, usually for God, from the Hebrew Bible (Old Testament) that often are applied to Jesus, too. I recently rediscovered an old poster that presented some of Jesus' names, and that rolled placard got me to thinking about the multiple possibilities for reflecting on and writing about the multiple names given to Jesus in the Bible. I have chosen to present fifty of them in this book. There are more than the fifty I have chosen; thus, this work is not exhaustive. Furthermore, the names chosen follow no particular format. So, the reader is free to jump around from one entry to another, from what catches his or her attention to the next attention grabber.

In our world, a name serves primarily to distinguish one person from another person. However, in the ancient world, a name often indicated a function. A name had a meaning; the meaning of a biblical name can be found in Bible dictionaries, commentaries, and footnotes today. Knowing someone's name gave the knower power over the one known. This is why God refuses to give Moses his name in the narrative of the burning bush, telling his chosen prophet that he is who he is (Exod 3:13–15). Thus, in the entries that follow I will give the meaning of a name for Jesus which often indicates one of his functions as understood by a biblical author.

The subtitle for this book is *Reflections for Advent and Christmas*. Often, both religious and spiritual people look for some reading material that will guide them through the Advent Season, usually three to four weeks long, and the Christmas Season, usually two to three weeks long. Many of the books written are based on a Lectionary, a book containing a predetermined set of biblical passages assigned for every day of Advent and Christmas. While I have written some of those Lectionary-based reflections in the past, I have chosen a more ecumenical approach here. I am hoping to appeal both to church-goers and to those who do not belong to any specific denomination. In other words, this book is general enough for any Christian.

Five-part Exercise

This book consists of exercises in fifteen-minute spirituality. Each of the fifty entries in this book offers selections organized into five parts which will provide the reader with about a fifteen-minute reflection on a name given to Jesus.

The first part is the name or title of the section.

The second part of each exercise is a short quotation from Scripture, which contains the mention of the name given in the title.

The reflection, part three, explores the meaning of the name in its biblical context in three paragraphs. It attempts to make some application for today. Each entry is thorough, readable, and to the point. It is built upon images the name evokes within its biblical book context, and it is designed to help the reader come to a deeper understanding of the name.

In the journal/meditation section, part four, the reader makes connections between the title, the Scripture passage, the reflection, and his or her own life. Those connections may be written in a journal—either paper or electronic—or meditated on with the help of the question. The journal/meditation question gets one started; where the journal/meditation goes cannot be predetermined. It may be a single statement or an idea with which one lingers for a few minutes, a few hours, or a few days. The process has no end; the reader decides when he or she has finished exploring the topic because he or she needs to attend to other things.

Once the reader is finished, the exercise is concluded with a short prayer, part five. The prayer summarizes the name announced in the title and Scripture, which was explored in the reflection, and which served as the foundation for the journal/meditation. Each prayer addresses Jesus using the name in the title of the entry and concludes with a Christian Trinitarian formula.

The five-part process is an exercise in spirituality, that is, growth in wisdom and grace. Spirituality, as a way of life, transforms, transfigures, the person step-by-step as he or she gets closer and closer to the divine—however one chooses to name it. After meeting the divine, the individual better understands some of the circumstances of his or her life, including his or her unique self. Spirituality is the way that one is in the divine's presence, which emerges through human experiences of biblical authors naming Jesus and guided reflections upon those experiences.

My hope is that you, the reader, will grow in spirituality throughout Advent and Christmas as you reflect on the names of Jesus. My prayer is that you will finish the spiritual journey of Advent and Christmas enriched for having spent time with the *Names for Jesus*.

Mark G. Boyer
Advent/Christmas 2016

Jesus

Scripture: ". . . [A]n angel of the Lord appeared to [Joseph] in a dream and said, 'Joseph, son of David, do not be afraid to take Mary as your wife, for the child conceived in her is from the Holy Spirit. She will bear a son, and you are to name him Jesus, for he will save his people from their sins.'" (Matt 1:20–21)

Reflection: In the Bible, the angel of the Lord is a code phrase for God. This can be seen in the story of Moses and the burning bush. The Exodus text is very clear that the angel of the LORD appeared to Moses in a flame of fire out of a bush (Exod 3:2). Then, the narrator of the story says that God called to him from the bush (Exod 3:4). So, Joseph, like Moses before him, is the recipient of direct divine revelation. Furthermore, his patriarchal namesake was a dreamer and an interpreter of dreams (Gen 37:1–41:57). God calls Joseph a son of David, because the narrator of Matthew's Gospel presents a spiritual genealogy of David's descendants conveniently arranged into three (the number for the divine) sets of fourteen (the sum of the letters in David) generations.

The angel directs Joseph to take pregnant Mary as his wife, even though the Law (Torah) dictates that he should expose her and have her stoned to death. Righteous Joseph redefines the meaning of righteousness; one who is righteous is not necessarily one who keeps Torah, but one who does the right thing because it is the right thing to do. At this point of Matthew's story, the author of the First Gospel is introducing his theme of higher righteousness. A person should not follow the Law just because it is the Torah; one should do what the Law intends, and sometimes that may mean breaking Torah to be declared righteous by God!

The point of all this is to get to the name. Again, the angel of the Lord—God—directs Joseph to name the son that Mary will bear Jesus. Jesus, the Greek form of Joshua—Moses' successor who saved the Israelites by leading them into the promised land by waging war and driving out the land's inhabitants—means "the Lord saves" or "Yahweh helps." Either way, Jesus for the author of Matthew's Gospel is the new Joshua, the new Moses, the man God helps. All of that is contained in the name Jesus, who delivers people from the Torah in order to instill in them a desire always to do the right thing because it is the right thing to do and because God wills such righteousness.

Journal/Meditation: What does the name Jesus mean to you? Which of the themes woven into the two verses from Matthew's Gospel most gets your attention? Why?

Prayer: Jesus, in your name I find salvation. Lead me through this life to the promised land of eternal life. Grant that your Father's angel may take this prayer to you where you live with him and the Holy Spirit, forever and ever. Amen.

Prince of Peace

Scripture: ". . . [A] child has been born for us, a son given to us; authority rests upon his shoulders; and he is named . . . Prince of Peace." (Isa 9:6)

Reflection: In chapter 9 of First Isaiah, the prophetic writer records a coronation hymn for a Davidic descendant. The kingdom of Judah in the south has been dominated by Assyrian rule; Judah's Davidic monarch has been a vassal king. Isaiah's coronation hymn looks to the new king—either Hezekiah or Josiah—of the royal house to untangle Judah from Assyria; Isaiah writes about this as a great light shining upon a people in darkness. The authority of the new king upon the throne will engender a return to national fortunes and prosperity.

It is impossible for modern readers to know if Isaiah is referring to King Hezekiah (716–687 BCE), successor of King Ahaz (735–716 BCE), or King Josiah (640–609 BCE). Hezekiah, who did repel the Assyrians, was not totally successful in overthrowing the overlords whose help his father had purchased to defend his kingdom from others. While Hezekiah did enact a literary renaissance and civil engineering works, it was Josiah who, after ending Assyrian control of Judah, initiates religious reform, repairing the Jerusalem temple and removing every sign of idolatry.

The coronation hymn names the new king—whoever he was—Prince of Peace. A prince is the son of a reigning monarch. In a country ruled by a king in the ancient world, a son was the hope for the future of the line which would guarantee security during his reign. For a small country dominated by Assyria, the king's son was the hope for freedom from war bringing serenity to squash anxiety. Harmony was the sought-after prize. When the name Prince of Peace is applied to Jesus, it becomes hyperbole, that is, deliberate and obvious exaggeration. He was not a prince insofar as he was not a son of a king; and he himself declared that he had not come to bring peace (Matt 10:34, Luke 12:51). However, to call Jesus the Prince of Peace is to mine a deep truth, namely that while the goal may be harmony, the way of life is often walking a road of warfare while clinging to the hope for serenity that only a son can give.

Journal/Meditation: What peace have you found while traveling the road of life? In the midst of life's trials, what has given you hope?

Prayer: Prince of Peace, the birth of a child gives me hope. Whatever authority may one day rest upon his or her shoulders will, hopefully, contribute to the betterment of the world. Increase within me the desire for harmony among all people that it may reflect the unity of you, Lord Jesus, with your Father and the Holy Spirit, one God, forever and ever. Amen.

Mighty God

Scripture: ". . . [A] child has been born for us, a son given to us; authority rests upon his shoulders; and he is named . . . Mighty God." (Isa 9:6)

Reflection: As indicated above, Isaiah's coronation hymn, probably written for King Hezekiah and then rewritten for King Josiah, refers to the monarch's heir as Prince of Peace. The oracle also names him Mighty God, a reference to the new king's power. The implied speaker of the coronation hymn is God's court, which declares that a child is born for the divine council. Ancient people presupposed that God had a court of various councilors just like kings did. Thus, the divine council joyously proclaims that the new king is a child of God born for all, a son of God given to all in the divine council.

When this name is applied to Jesus, it quickly turns the man into God. Indeed, John's Gospel states this explicitly when the author declares that "the Word was with God, and the Word was God" in the beginning (John 1:1). This Word "became flesh and lived among us" (John 1:14). And while he lived among us, this Mighty God enacted signs of mighty deeds in order to spark faith in those who saw and heard him. While he works many mighty deeds in John's Gospel, he gives seven major signs that reveal his glory "as of a father's only son, full of grace and truth" (John 1:14).

Many people think of only the LORD when the phrase Mighty God is spoken. The prophet Isaiah's coronation hymn applies it to the son of the king who wields his father's or his Father's power. Christians have applied Isaiah's words to Jesus in order to declare him to be the Father's only Son, the one who reveals heavenly glory on earth through his powerful words and deeds.

Journal/Meditation: What does the name Mighty God mean to you? What are the implications of your meaning(s)?

Prayer: Mighty God, only Son of the Father, you were in the beginning with God. In you were life and light. Grant that I may shine brightly with your grace and lead others to you, who live and reign with the Father and the Holy Spirit, one God, forever and ever. Amen.

Wonderful Counselor

Scripture: ". . . [A] child has been born for us, a son given to us; authority rests upon his shoulders; and he is named Wonderful Counselor." (Isa 9:6)

Reflection: Isaiah's coronation hymn, sometimes referred to as an oracle, uses the metaphor of birth. When the prophet writes that a child has been born, he is not referring literally to a male heir; the birth is a metaphor for the coronation service. The son of the king enters the service as a prince and leaves it as a king; he is born again. By passing through the ceremony—which serves as a birth canal—the child becomes a son of God who is given the authority to rule God's people.

Psalm 2 illustrates this best. This song, most likely used during the coronation ceremony for Judean kings, presents the new king announcing the decree of the LORD. God says to the new king: "You are my son; today I have begotten you" (Ps 2:7). Like Isaiah's divine council that accepts the new king as God's son, Psalm 2 portrays the LORD directly stating that the new king is his son. And the day of his coronation is the day of his begetting or birth as such! The new king is titled Wonderful Counselor to stress his wisdom in offering advice in the act of ruling his kingdom.

When this title is transferred to Jesus, as the author of John's Gospel does indirectly in the prologue, the counselor was "in the beginning with God. All things came into being through him, and without him not one thing came into being" (John 1:2–3a). The author of the Fourth Gospel is echoing personified Wisdom's words in the Book of Proverbs. The Wonderful Counselor, that is,

Wisdom, declares: "The LORD created me at the beginning of his work, the first of his acts of long ago. Ages ago I was set up, at the first, before the beginning of the earth. . . . I was beside him, like a master worker" (Prov 8:22–23, 30a). One who offers wisdom to another does so from the depths of his or her personal experiences of life lived in relationship with God.

Journal/Meditation: What authentic, wonderful counsel have you offered to another? Who was it? What lived, personal experiences of God did you draw upon to share your wisdom?

Prayer: Wonderful Counselor, through your words and deeds you have revealed to me the wisdom of God. Guide me with your Holy Spirit to even deeper levels of reflection upon the events of my life living in relationship with the Father that I may reveal your wisdom to others. You live and reign as one God forever and ever. Amen.

Everlasting Father

Scripture: ". . . [A] child has been born for us, a son given to us; authority rests upon his shoulders; and he is named . . . Everlasting Father." (Isa 9:6)

Reflection: The name Everlasting Father does not refer to God in Isaiah's oracle. The name is given to the new king to express hope that his reign will prove him to be the father and protector of his people. The prophet states that the new king's authority will grow and result in endless peace in his kingdom. That authority will be supported with justice and righteousness (Isa 9:7). In other words, the new king will treat his subjects with fairness while observing the religious and moral code of Torah.

Such hyperbolic coronation language is typical of enthronement hymns. The Davidic heir represents the epitome of hope for the future for Isaiah, as well as for many other prophets. Intangible hope becomes tangible in the person of the new king, heralded as a son of God and anointed as such. All of the nation's dreams are projected onto him. He—no matter if he were Hezekiah or Josiah—becomes the incarnation of hope for a better future, no matter how human he will also be!

It is not difficult to see why this title of Everlasting Father is applied to Jesus. As a spiritual descendent of David, he is anointed by the Holy Spirit at his baptism, mentioned by all four gospel writers (Mark 1:10, Matt 3:16, Luke 3:22, John 1:32–33). Likewise, the voice that comes from heaven, the voice of God, declares him to be his son (Mark 1:11, Matt 3:17, Luke 3:22) or John the Baptist does so (John 1:34). His mission is to proclaim the kingdom of God, to announce how much God loves people and desires to protect them. Jesus is the incarnation of hope. Intangible hope now becomes tangible in the person of Jesus, called the Christ (meaning anointed), heralded as the son of God. All of every human's dreams are projected onto him. He becomes the incarnation of hope for a better future, no matter how human he must also be!

Journal/Meditation: How is Jesus Christ an Everlasting Father to you? In what specific ways have you experienced him protecting you, using his authority with justice and righteousness to proclaim God's kingdom to you?

Prayer: Everlasting Father, throughout your reign you are the father and protector of all people as you proclaim God's kingdom. Grant me the grace to hope for the fullness of the kingdom in which all love is manifest. You live and reign with the Father and the Holy Spirit forever and ever. Amen.

Holy One

Scripture: Jesus and his four disciples "went to Capernaum; and when the sabbath came he entered the synagogue and taught. They were astounded at his teaching, for he taught them as one having authority, and not as the scribes. Just then there was in their synagogue a man with an unclean spirit, and he cried out, 'What have you to do with us, Jesus of Nazareth? Have you come to destroy us? I know who you are, the Holy One of God.'" (Mark 1:21–24)

Reflection: The Markan Jesus has just called four boat owners from Capernaum to follow him. Entering the synagogue, a place where the local Jewish community assembles for worship on the sabbath, Jesus, who is not a teacher, teaches with more authority than the scribes, who were trained in the interpretation of the Torah or Law. Not only is that enough to amaze the assembly, but it causes a man with an unclean spirit to step forward. The reader is not told what kind of demon this nameless man possesses or is possessed by, but this is the first of many such exorcisms the author of Mark's Gospel will portray Jesus doing.

The astonishment of the crowd at Jesus' teaching is surpassed by the never-truer words spoken by the demoniac. The possessed man declares Jesus to be the Holy One of God. However, as will be seen by reading more of Mark's Gospel, the disciples—four at this point in the story—never recognize who Jesus is while the possessed, the ill, and the unclean do. In this book, the author portrays the all-knowing demons presenting the truth that the ignorant disciples can never comprehend. With its knowledge, this unclean spirit attempts to gain control over Jesus in order to resist being driven out of its host. However, the demon's move fails. The Holy One of God is the opposite of the uncleanness of the spirit. Thus, the Markan Jesus, exercising all the holiness that the unclean spirit has attributed to him, commands the spirit to be silent and come out. Once this occurs, the crowd is amazed (Mark 1:25–27).

This naming of Jesus as the Holy One of God and his exorcism of the unclean spirit introduces a theme woven throughout Mark's Gospel: Who is Jesus? Biblical scholars refer to this theme as the messianic secret, a phrase the author of the work does not employ. The basic theme is that the Markan Jesus tells unclean spirits and disciples not to reveal his identity as he, the herald of God's kingdom, engages with the powers that oppose God. To name Jesus the Holy One is also to join in this two-fold work: proclaim the kingdom while battling all who oppose its breaking into the world.

Journal/Meditation: Do you think that Jesus is the Holy One of God? If so, in what specific ways do you proclaim God's kingdom while casting out unclean spirits? If not, what truth do you declare to others?

Prayer: Holy One of God, your battle with everything opposed to your Father came to an end on your cross. The sign of your defeat was in all truth the sign of God's victory through you. Give me the strength of grace and fill me with the wisdom of the Spirit that I may have the courage to proclaim God's kingdom while battling whatever is opposed to it. You live and reign forever and ever. Amen.

Lamb of God

Scripture: "The next day [John] saw Jesus coming toward him and declared, 'Here is the Lamb of God who takes away the sin of the world!'" (John 1:29)

Reflection: The author of John's Gospel often steps out of his storytelling shoes and directly addresses the reader of the work. This narrative technique—often portrayed with italics in books and voices out of nowhere or words on the screen in films—is designed to draw the reader more deeply into the story and sometimes to give the reader important information which none of the other characters have in the account. So, at this point in John's Gospel John the Baptist tells the reader that Jesus is the Lamb of God. John repeats this scenario a few verses later when he and two of his disciples watch Jesus walk by and John the Baptist declares to them, "Look, here is the Lamb of God!" (John 1:35)

John's naming of Jesus as the Lamb of God is intended to get the reader to remember the last plague in the Book of Exodus

(11:1–12:36). The Hebrews are instructed by God through Moses to roast a lamb after smearing its blood on the lintel and doorposts of their home. When the LORD passes over the land of Egypt, he will see the blood and not strike dead the first-born of those who hold his people in slavery. The blood of the lamb saves the Hebrews; the death of the first-born spurs pharaoh to release the slaves.

For the author of John's Gospel, Jesus is the new passover lamb; his blood on the cross sets free people from whatever keeps them from entering into a deep relationship with God. The author of this gospel picks up this theme again when he states that "it was the day of Preparation for the Passover" (John 19:14) when Jesus is crucified and dies at the same time as the passover lambs were being slaughtered in the temple. He alludes to this again when he declares that Jesus' legs were not broken, as were those of the two co-crucified criminals. "None of his bones shall be broken" (John 19:36) is meant to echo Exodus 12:46 and Numbers 9:12; both are passages detailing the preparation of the passover lamb. Thus, according to John's Gospel, the body of Jesus replaces the passover lamb that once saved the Hebrews from death; Jesus' death bestows upon all people eternal life.

Journal/Meditation: From what death has Jesus rescued you? What new life have you experienced as a result of being rescued from death?

Prayer: Lamb of God, you take away the sins of the world and offer all people eternal life. Grant that I may repeatedly celebrate the passover through death to new life so I may share in your merciful and eternal life. You live and reign with the Father and the Holy Spirit, one God, forever and ever. Amen.

Author (Prince) of Life

Scripture: Peter addressed the Jews, saying: "... [Y]ou rejected the Holy and Righteous One and asked to have a murderer given to you, and you killed the Author of life, whom God raised from the dead. To this we are witnesses.'" (Acts 3:14–15)

Reflection: Most biblical translations of Acts 3:15 refer to Jesus as the Author of life, while some translations call him the Prince of life. The Greek word can also mean the leader of life, the pioneer of life, the one who opens the way to life. The author of the Acts of Apostles—understood to be the same writer of Luke's Gospel—is not attributing the invention of human life to Jesus, but is declaring him to be the founder of eternal life, salvation, by God's raising him from the dead. Because he was the first to rise from the dead, Jesus is the Author of life, the Prince of life.

The context for this title in the Acts of the Apostles is the healing of a lame man by Peter and John at the Beautiful Gate of the Temple. After the healing has occurred, Peter addresses the crowd of observers, declaring that it was the God of their ancestors who healed the lame man, just as that same God raised Jesus from the dead (Acts 3:12–13). It was this Jesus that they rejected and handed over to Pilate, echoing Luke 23:20–24. Peter continues to denounce his hearers for their role in rejecting the Holy and Righteous One, especially for asking for the release of a murderer, again echoing Luke 23:18–19, 25. Peter then tells his Jewish audience—those who deal in death—that they killed the Author of life, the Prince of life, but God—who deals in life—raised Jesus from the dead. In other words, God is the antithesis of death as demonstrated in Jesus' resurrection.

Peter and John are witnesses to God's power to give new life. According to Peter, God can trump death with life in the resurrection of Jesus, the Author of life, the Prince of life, the leader of life, the pioneer of life, the one who opens the way to new life. Furthermore, the healing of the lame man at the word of Peter and John is due to his faith in the name of Jesus. Faith in his name becomes the agency of the same divine power that raised the Author (Prince) of life from the dead.

Journal/Meditation: What new life has your faith in the name of Jesus brought you? Using a specific experience, apply the title of Author (Prince) of life to it. What further insight do you now have?

Prayer: Author of life, your God rejected those who ignored you, the Holy and Righteous One, by raising you from the dead and making you the Prince of life. Grant that my experiences of new life will enable me to be your witness. You live and reign with the Father and the Holy Spirit, one God, forever and ever. Amen.

Lord God Almighty

Scripture: "[Seven angels with harps of God in their hands] sing the song of Moses, the servant of God, and the song of the Lamb: 'Great and amazing are your deeds, Lord God the Almighty! Just and true are your ways, King of the nations!'" (Rev 15:3)

Reflection: The song of Moses and the song of the Lamb sung by the seven angels with God's harps is composed from other biblical hymns and presented as a mosaic of Hebrew Bible (Old Testament) phrases. Part of the new song comes from the song Moses and the Israelites sing after passing safely through the Red Sea and escaping the Egyptian army (Exod 15:1). Another part of the new song comes from the Book of Deuteronomy in which Moses recites the words of a forty-three verse song (Deut 32:4). Other parts of the song come from Psalms 111:2, 139:14, 145:17, 86:8–9, and 98:2 along with the prophets Jeremiah 10:6–7 and 16:19, Amos 4:13, and Malachi 1:11. The purpose of the new song is to portray those who sing it as being committed both to Moses and to Jesus because they have been delivered from the beast.

Both God and Jesus are given the name Lord God the Almighty in some translations or Lord God Almighty in other translations of the hymn of praise. Lord refers to authority, the power to command. God refers to a divine being. And Almighty refers to having supreme, unquestionable power over everything. Thus, the name indicates that both God and Jesus are divine beings possessing supreme power over the whole world and everything in it. That is why the name King of the Nations is added to the hymn. A king possesses supreme power over all he rules.

This reflection may come as a shock to those bible readers who have absorbed the psychological notion of modern times that a person is in absolute charge of his or her future. Self-actualization is not a biblical concept! The biblical concept is that the Lord God Almighty is in charge of everything, and that all his creatures can do is praise him for his amazing deeds, for his just and true ways. The choices presented by these two perspectives are these: a person can submit to the all-powerful God or to the all-powerful self.

Journal/Meditation: What does calling Jesus Lord God Almighty mean to you? How do you reconcile the biblical world's perspective and the modern world's perspective?

Prayer: Lord God Almighty, great and amazing are your deeds. Just and true are all your ways, King of the Nations. Only your holy name is worthy to be glorified. Grant that all nations will come and worship you, Father, Son, and Holy Spirit, one God, forever and ever. Amen.

Lion of the Tribe of Judah

Scripture: ". . . [O]ne of the elders said . . . , 'Do not weep. See, the Lion of the tribe of Judah, the Root of David, has conquered, so that he can open the scroll and its seven seals.'" (Rev 5:5)

Reflection: This scene in the Book of Revelation begins with God seated on his throne holding a seven-sealed scroll in his right hand. The scroll represents secret knowledge. The detail of it being held in God's right hand indicates that not only is the one who holds the scroll powerful, but that the scroll itself possesses powerful words. The number of its seals—wax that has been impressed with the writer's mark or sign—indicates that its contents are perfect, containing God's will. There is only one who can accept the scroll, break its seals, and read it: the Lion of the Tribe of Judah.

In the patriarch Jacob's farewell speech before his death, he addresses his son Judah as "a lion's whelp." He sates, "He crouches down, he stretches out like a lion, like a lioness—who dares rouse him up?" (Gen 49:9) The name Lion of the Tribe of Judah was the Jewish expected savior, the one who would rescue the people from their foreign overlords. Because it comes from the Hebrew word Messiah, meaning anointed, Christians applied the name to Jesus, whom they believe to be the anointed, the Lion of the Tribe of Judah.

The Lion of the Tribe of Judah is the Lamb in the Book of Revelation. Even though he has been slaughtered (crucified), he possesses perfect power (seven horns) and perfect knowledge (seven eyes). The lion is the antithesis of the lamb! And yet he is the only one who can take the scroll and, by disclosing its contents, make its words come to pass. Power is not found in the lion, but it is found in the lamb, the definitive name for Jesus in the Book of Revelation. The lamb got his power and knowledge through the cross. God's power and knowledge are now transferred to him through the scroll.

Journal/Meditation: In what specific ways have you achieved power and knowledge (lion) through weakness (lamb)? Why is the name Lion of the Tribe of Judah appropriate for Jesus? Why is the designation of Lamb appropriate for Jesus?

Prayer: Lion of the Tribe of Judah, you conquered death with life and earned the right to open the scroll and its seven seals. Grant me the power and knowledge to entrust my life to your mercy and care. I hope to surround your throne and praise you, who live and reign with the Father and the Holy Spirit, forever and ever. Amen.

Root of David

Scripture: "It is I, Jesus, who sent my angel to you with this testimony for the churches. I am the root and the descendant of David . . . ." (Rev 22:16)

Reflection: Giving Jesus the name Root of David applies a messianic image to him. At the time of Jesus, the Jews expected an anointed one of God, a Messiah, who would deliver them from their foreign oppressors and restore the ruler of Judah, that is, the King of Judah. The line of Judah's kings could trace its lineage all the way back to David. The Jewish messianic hope was a physical impossibility—baring any direct intervention by the LORD God— since the line of Judah had ended with the Babylonian deportation in 587 BCE. To name Jesus the Root of David is to make a Christian claim about him that the Jews could never make!

Thus, when the OT (A) Book of Sirach states that the LORD "gave a remnant to Jacob, and to David a root from his own family" (Sir 47:22c), the author is reemphasizing the belief that the Davidic line would never be destroyed; a physical descendent of Judah's most important king would always sit on his throne. The prophet Isaiah also emphasized this belief in an eternal covenant, writing that a shoot would come from "the stump of Jesse, and a branch [would] grow out of his roots (Isa 11:1). Since Jesse was David's father, "the root of Jesse [would] stand as a signal to the peoples; the nations [would] inquire of him, and his dwelling [would] be glorious" (Isa 11:10). In his Letter to the Romans, Paul uses Isaiah 11:10 to demonstrate how God has now made it possible for the Gentiles to glorify God as his people alongside the Jews.

The author of the Book of Revelation, pseudonymously known as John of Patmos, refers to Jesus as the Root of David one other time in Revelation 5:5, where he is also called the Lion of the Tribe of Judah. By the time of the writing of the Christian Bible (New Testament), the Jewish hope for a political Messiah (anointed one) had been turned into the Christian belief that Jesus was the spiritual Messiah who fulfilled all expectations stemming from God's promise. While he did not overthrow the Roman oc-cupation forces in his own country, Christians claim that he was God's anointed. Thus, he is named the Root of David.

Journal/Meditation: How do you understand the name Root of David? In what ways does Jesus not fulfill Jewish expectations? How has Christianity changed the meaning of Root of David?

Prayer: Root of David, through your resurrection from the dead, you gave new meaning to the expectation of a Messiah from the Root of Jesse. Help me recognize that you, Jesus, sent your angel with this testimony for the churches dedicated to you around the world. You live and reign with the Father and the Holy Spirit, one God, forever and ever. Amen.

Word of Life

Scripture: "We declare to you what was from the beginning, what we have heard, what we have seen with our eyes, what we have looked at and touched with our hands, concerning the word of life." (1 John 1:1)

Reflection: The opening of the First Letter of John borrows themes from John's Gospel that first emphasize the humanity of Jesus. It is not difficult to detect this letter's dependence upon the gospel. Both begin in the beginning (John 1:1, 1 John 1:1). Both mention what has been heard, that is the message, the Word (John 1:1, 1 John 1:1). Both emphasize seeing (John 1:6–9, 1 John 1:1) and looking and touching (John 1:6–9, 1 John 1:1). The word of life refers both to the message and the person of Jesus, who, according to John's Gospel, was the Word (John 1:1) and the life (John 1:4).

According to Johannine thought, the Word—both the mes-sage and the person—reveals eternal life. This life was with the Father, but it has now been revealed (1 John 1:2, John 1:18). In other words, eternal life is presented as a personified entity. In the words of John's Gospel, the word became flesh and lived on earth; people saw his glory. It was the glory as of a father's only son, full of grace and truth (John 1:14). The incarnation was, thus, an historical event according to the First Letter of John. Thus, the title Word of Life for Jesus serves as a double entendre; it means that he as God bore the Holy One's life into the world and that he as man was the embodiment of that very life. A third understanding is also possible, namely, the word that Jesus spoke while he was on earth was the Word of Life.

Jesus is unique among humankind because, according to the First Letter of John, he was the physical revelation of the invisible God who brought God's life into the world and spoke about that life in his words and deeds. While that is a lot for anyone to understand, it reveals the depths of the Johannine author's identification of Jesus. In his very person he was the physical revelation of the invisible God to those who could hear, see, and touch.

Journal/Meditation: What life do you experience as eternal? How is Jesus a revelation of eternal life for you? What specific words of Jesus charge you with eternal life?

Prayer: Word of Life, who was with God from the beginning, I have heard you, seen you with my eyes, looked at you, and touched you with my hands. Grant that your word takes root in me and reveals the eternal life that was with the Father that I may share in it now and forever and ever. Amen.

Author and Finisher of Our Faith

Scripture: "Therefore, since we are surrounded by so great a cloud of witnesses, let us also lay aside every weight and the sin that clings so closely, and let us run with perseverance the race that is set before us, looking to Jesus the pioneer and perfecter of our faith, who for the sake of the joy that was set before him endured the cross, disregarding its shame, and has taken his seat at the right hand of the throne of God." (Heb 12:1–2)

Reflection: Some biblical translations name Jesus as the Author and Finisher of Our Faith, while others declare him to be the Pioneer and Perfecter of Our Faith or the Leader and Perfecter of Our Faith. Each of these translations adds its own spin on the meaning of the name. For example, the first term of each pair, that is, author, implies that Jesus is the founder of all those in the cloud of witnesses; pioneer implies that he is the initiator of faith, having attained its goal; and leader implies that he is out in front running faith's race.

The second term of each pair also offers different connotations. For example, finisher implies that Jesus has completed the race through crucifixion and won the race by resurrection; now he is seated at God's right hand in power. Naming Jesus perfecter does not imply the content of Christian belief, but the trust in God that he exhibited and in which his followers are called upon to share. In other words, Jesus perfectly embodies faith and is the model for all to follow.

Basically, Hebrews presents Jesus as the ideal example. He paid no attention to the shame of the cross; he completed his life's mission walking through his suffering rather than attempting to walk around it. Because of his faithfulness, God vindicated him by raising him from the dead and seating him at the Father's right hand. Thus, he is author, pioneer, and leader; he is finisher and perfecter of faithfulness placed in God, who raises the dead.

Journal/Meditation: What do these pairs of names for Jesus mean to you: Author and Finisher of Our Faith, Pioneer and Perfecter of Our Faith, and Leader and Perfecter of Our Faith? How is Jesus a model of faithfulness to God for you?

Prayer: Author and Perfecter of Our Faith, you have surrounded me with a great cloud of witnesses from the past who urge me to run with perseverance the race of faith. As my model, Jesus, keep before my eyes the joy of your kingdom that I may endure my life's suffering and come to participate in the glory you share with the Father and the Holy Spirit forever and ever. Amen.

Advocate

Scripture: "My little children, I am writing these things to you so that you may not sin. But if anyone does sin, we have an advocate with the Father, Jesus Christ, the righteous." (1 John 2:1)

Reflection: Naming Jesus Advocate—in Greek Paraclete—implies that he is a helper or advisor. In John's Gospel, the Paraclete sayings are about the Holy Spirit (John 14:16, 26; 15:26; 16:7). Uniquely in the First Letter of John, Jesus is named the Paraclete or Advocate. In other words, Jesus is like a lawyer who represents sinners before God.

In John 14:16, Jesus promises to ask the Father to send his followers "another Advocate," another Paraclete, implying that he is an Advocate or Paraclete. In John's Gospel, the meaning is similar to that presented in the First Letter of John. But that is where the similarity ends. Throughout John's Gospel, the Advocate is the active helper in the lives of disciples, the equivalent of the Holy Spirit, who bridges the time between Christ's departure and the end. The gospel's Advocate secures continuity from Jesus throughout history. The First Letter of John's Advocate presents Jesus as the mediator or intercessor with God for those who sin.

From time to time, everyone needs a helper, one who assists another in some way big or small. From time to time, everyone needs a mediator, one who brings opposites into harmony. And from time to time, everyone needs an intercessor, one who pleads on another's behalf. In naming Jesus Advocate, we identify him as the one who assists us, bringing us into God's presence, and pleading God's mercy for us.

Journal/Meditation: In what specific ways has Jesus helped you? What opposites has he brought into harmony in your life? What mercy has he obtained from God for you?

Prayer: Advocate, when I sin, you plead with the Father to shower mercy upon me. Assist me in my daily life with your face-to-face intercessory presence with God. And grant that I may one day participate in the glory you share with the Father and the Holy Spirit forever and ever. Amen.

The Way

Scripture: Jesus said to his disciples: "'. . . [Y]ou know the way to the place where I am going.' Thomas said to him, 'Lord, we do not know where you are going. How can we know the way?' Jesus said to him, 'I am the way . . . . No one comes to the Father except through me.'" (John 14:4–6)

Reflection: Before Jesus' incarnation, the way to God was through observance of the Torah. The six hundred thirteen precepts of the Law that God gave to Moses on Mount Sinai (Horeb) presented in detail everything that was to be done and everything that was to be avoided in order to achieve holiness. However, as Jesus does many times in John's Gospel, he replaces something in Judaism with himself. He declares that he is the new way to God.

Using the divine name, I AM, in a double-entendre sense, he states that he himself (man) is the way to God, and that he himself (God) is the way to God! He came from God and was going to God (John 8:42, 16:27). It is easier to imagine a road that is paved from earth to the world above. If we name that road Jesus and travel over it (him), it leads us to God. All we have to do is walk on it. That is what naming Jesus The Way means. No one can get to God, according to the Johannine Jesus, except through him.

Like Thomas, we may find ourselves declaring that we do not know the way because we do not know where Jesus went. And sometimes we take side roads that lead us nowhere. Other times we may get lost and need to be found. Our assistance comes from a compass, the Holy Spirit, who points us in the right direction if we seek spiritual guidance. Life is, indeed, a journey, but death does not end it. We continue on the way to God through Jesus, The Way.

Journal/Meditation: In what specific experiences of your life has Jesus been a way to God for you? How was the Holy Spirit like a compass pointing you in the right direction?

Prayer: The Way, I often do not know the place to which I am going. So, I must rely upon you to be the way with the guidance of your Holy Spirit. Throughout my life journey, keep me on the road that leads to the Father, who with you and the Holy Spirit are one God forever and ever. Amen.

The Truth

Scripture: Jesus said to his disciples: "'. . . [Y]ou know the way to the place where I am going.' Thomas said to him, 'Lord, we do not know where you are going. How can we know the way?' Jesus said to him, 'I am . . . the truth . . . . No one comes to the Father except through me.'" (John 14:4–6)

Reflection: Before Jesus' incarnation, the truth of God was found in the Torah. The six hundred thirteen precepts of the Law that God gave to Moses on Mount Sinai (Horeb) presented in detail everything that was to be done and everything that was to be avoided in order to plumb the depths of truth. However, as the narrator of John's Gospel states, "The law indeed was given through Moses; grace and truth came through Jesus Christ" (John 1:17). Just as he does with The Way, so does Jesus replace the truth of the Torah with himself. He declares that he is the new truth of God. He tells a group of Jews that if they continue in his word, they will know the truth and the truth will make them free (John 8:31–32).

John's Gospel declares Jesus to be "full of grace and truth" (John 1:14); he proclaims God's word to be truth (John 17:17). He tells a group of Jews that he is a man who tells them the truth that he heard from God (John 8:40). In the passage above, he uses the divine name, I AM, to declare that he himself is God's incarnate truth. While truth usually means conformity with fact or reality as experienced, biblical truth means conformity with God and God's perspective as conveyed in the biblical text.

For example, biblical truth is often ambiguous. There are two different stories of creation truth. The two books of Kings are re-written as the two books of Chronicles. There are four gospels, and each one of them presents a different portrait of Jesus. Thus, biblical truth needs to be navigated. It is like knowing the truth about one's self. While it sets one free to be his or her unique, unrepeatable incarnation of God's truth, it also means that God's truth is plural and beyond our ability to comprehend it totally. Naming Jesus The Truth in John's Gospel is but one of many different truths.

Journal/Meditation: What biblical truth do you find ambiguous? How does that biblical truth enrich the perspective of your life?

Prayer: The Truth, you are the source of all grace and truth that comes from the Father. Fill me with a thirst for divine truth that I may know it and be set free to serve you. You live and reign as one God—Father, Son, and Holy Spirit—forever and ever. Amen.

The Life

Scripture: Jesus said to his disciples: "'. . . [Y]ou know the way to the place where I am going.' Thomas said to him, 'Lord, we do not know where you are going. How can we know the way?' Jesus said to him, 'I am . . . the life. No one comes to the Father except through me.'" (John 14:4–6)

Reflection: Before the Johannine Jesus declared himself to be the life observance of Torah's six hundred thirteen precepts was the way of life. The Law God gave to Moses on Mount Sinai (Horeb) stipulated how one lived life in relationship with God for hundreds of years. As he does repeatedly in John's Gospel, Jesus replaces the old way of life with a new one: himself.

In the passage above, Jesus uses life as a double-entendre. He understands life as lived now, the earthly life experienced from birth to death on the planet named Earth. However, he also understands life to be on the other side of death, labeled eternal life. After a person walks through death, life is changed; it is not ended. Jesus replaces both life on this side of death and life on the other side of death with himself. He is the life of God, often called grace. On earth he is the incarnate or embodied God, who exists as disembodied spirit in heaven.

Using I AM, the divine name God games Moses on Mount Horeb (Sinai) (Exod 3:14), the Johannine Jesus declares that God is life and that he (God) is life. Daily human existence, named life, is not all there is. Naming Jesus as The Life means that daily life is already an experience of eternal life, the fullness of which will only be revealed on the other side of death.

Journal/Meditation: In what specific ways does Jesus give life to you? Where do you find traces of eternal life in your daily life right now?

Prayer: The Life, you who existed from the beginning, you became incarnate and lived among us. Through your death and resurrection, you revealed the life that exists and awaits me on the other side of death. Grant me the grace to be able to recognize and live life fully now while awaiting its eternity after my death. You live and reign with the Father and the Holy Spirit, one God, forever and ever. Amen.

Dayspring

Scripture: "By the tender mercy of our God, the dawn from on high will break upon us, to give light to those who sit in darkness and in the shadow of death, to guide our feet into the way of peace." (Luke 1:77–78)

Reflection: Dayspring, meaning the first light of day, is considered archaic English usage. That is why modern biblical translations now render it as dawn from on high. Either is an attempt to capture the first, barely-visible, streak of light that appears on the eastern horizon. Daybreak, the beginning of a new day with the sun's rays creeping over the eastern sky, evokes hope in those who watch and wait in the late hours of the night into the early hours of the day. The prophet Malachi referred to the dayspring as the sun of righteousness (Mal 4:2). The sun promises liberation from any kind of darkness. The sun does what it is supposed to do, according to ancient cosmology; it rises every day and shines on those who have been sitting in darkness and death.

The passage above comes from the canticle recited by Zechariah after his son, John the Baptist, was named and circumcised. The words do not refer to John, but they predict the one whom John will proclaim. Zechariah praises God for the blessing of light which he identifies as a tender mercy of God. In other words, God gives an undeserved gift of light to those in darkness and death. God demonstrates kindness that goes beyond what justice requires, that goes beyond what can be expected.

Naming Jesus the Dayspring, that is, the dawn from on high, proclaims him to be the new light of God streaming onto the earth, much like the sun's rays shine upon the earth. The dark shadows of the past are dispelled. John the Baptist will herald the work of the one arising who himself represents the manifestation of the compassion of God. The result of the Dayspring will be peace, a state of harmony of people living in relationship with their God.

Journal/Meditation: What do the first streaks of dawn in the eastern sky do for you? How is a new day a gift to you from God's box of tender mercies?

Prayer: Dayspring, like the first rays of a new day you have spread the light of God upon the earth. Grant me the gift of insight to walk without stumbling during this life in the hope of dwelling in eternal light with you and the Father and the Holy Spirit forever and ever. Amen.

Lord of All

Scripture: "Then Peter began to speak to [Cornelius and his household]: 'I truly understand that God shows no partiality, but in every nation anyone who fears him and does what is right is acceptable to him. You know the message he sent to the people of Israel, preaching peace by Jesus Christ—he is Lord of all.'" (Acts 10:34–36)

Reflection: The above passage comes from the longer narrative of Peter visiting the home of the Roman centurion Cornelius after both have experienced visions directing that they meet each other. Commonly referred to as the Gentile Pentecost—to distinguish it from the Jewish Pentecost in Acts 2:1–13—the descent of the Holy Spirit upon Cornelius and his household launches the mission to the Gentiles, just as the descent of the Holy Spirit as wind, tongues, fire, and language launched the mission to the Jews. Peter's insight about God showing no partiality to any specific group of people leads him to declare Jesus to be Lord of All. This is an earth-shaking event, because the Jews believed that they were the chosen people. Had God now changed his mind? Furthermore, God had sent a message of peace through Jesus Christ (Luke 1:79, 2:14, 7:50, 8:48, 10:5–6, 19:38, 24:36) to all the nations; this meant to Jews and Gentiles.

Peter's declaration that Jesus is Lord of All refers to his exaltation, which Peter speaks about immediately after the Jewish Pentecost. (Acts 2:34–36). Naming Jesus Lord of All signifies power and authority in both the Jewish and the Gentile world. Luke, the author of the Acts of the Apostles, portrays Peter abandoning his own Jewish perspective in order to understand and present a universal point of view. In the language of the Acts, Peter begins to grasp God's work that has occurred in Jesus (Acts 10:38). That is why after Peter finishes speaking to Cornelius and his household the Holy Spirit falls upon all the Gentiles present. All are then baptized (Acts 10:44–48).

Naming Jesus Lord of All has consequences. One's world view must be expanded from the usual narrow perspective to a universal one. Peter's perspective opens from Jewish to Gentile to all-encompassing. Churches can isolate themselves in doctrinal differences instead of opening their doors to all people. Instead of seeing their differences as enriching, some people reject others because of their lifestyle, tattoos, length of hair, and on and on. According to Peter, Jesus came to erase the narrow world view and teach all people about the universal one, which is God's perspective.

Journal/Meditation: What specific issues keep your narrow perspective and keep you from a more universal point of view? How can you remove those from your view?

Prayer: Lord of All, your God shows no partiality. Anyone in any nation who fears him and does what is right is acceptable to him. Through you he sent his message of peace to all people. Grant me that peace in this life and in the life to come. You, Jesus Christ, are Lord of All forever and ever. Amen.

I AM

Scripture: "Jesus said to [the Jews], 'Very truly, I tell you, before Abraham was, I am.'" (John 8:58)

Reflection: In his dialogue with some Jews, the Johannine Jesus identifies himself with God by employing the name God gave to Moses. After experiencing the LORD in a flame of fire out of a bush that was not consumed, Moses asks God for his name, and God replies, "I AM WHO I AM" (Exod 3:14). The God who is who he is also causes to be. This divine name, sometimes rendered Yahweh, is not pronounced. Even to this day, biblical texts substitute Adonai (LORD) in its place. In giving his name to Moses, God reveals that he encompasses all time in himself and that he is existence or being itself.

When Jesus tells the Jews "I Am," he is claiming the divine name for himself. He is saying that he is God. This is why they immediately accuse him of blasphemy and pick up stones to kill him (John 8:59). Throughout John's Gospel, Jesus employs the divine name in what have come to be called the I AM sayings. He declares that he is the bread of life, the sustenance of his followers (John 6:35); the light of the world which scatters darkness (John 8:12, 9:5); the gate through which people get to God (John 19:7, 9); the good shepherd who guides and protects his follower-sheep (John 10:11, 14); the resurrection of the dead and the one who bestows eternal life (John 11:25); the vine, the source of all life for the branches connected to him (John 15:1, 5); and the way, the truth, and the life (John 14:6), as already examined above.

This unique Johannine usage suggests that Jesus is not only God, but that he replaces all the former Jewish images of God. If the LORD fed his people with manna in the desert, Jesus now feeds them with his body and blood. If the LORD was light, Jesus is now light. If the LORD was the gate, Jesus now serves that purpose. If the LORD was shepherd of his people, Jesus now claims that role for himself. If the LORD planted the vine of his people Israel, Jesus now is the vine from whom all branches are nourished. Naming

Jesus I AM means that through the incarnate one people have been given direct access to God.

Journal/Meditation: Which I AM saying gets most of your attention? What does it mean to you? How does it draw you closer to God?

Prayer: Before Abraham was, you were, I AM. Through your incarnation, you have revealed the Father, who gave his name to Moses in the burning bush. You have declared yourself to be the bread of life, the light of the world, the gate, the good shepherd, the resurrection and the life, the way, the truth, and the life, and the vine that connects all the branches to the LORD. Grant me a share in this abundant mercy. You are God with the Father and the Holy Spirit forever and ever. Amen.

Son of God

Scripture: ". . . John [the Baptist] testified, 'I saw the Spirit descending from heaven like a dove, and it remained on [Jesus]. I myself did not know him, but the one who sent me to baptize with water said to me, "He on whom you see the Spirit descend and remain is the one who baptizes with the Holy Spirit." And I myself have seen and have testified that this is the Son of God.'" (John 1:32–34)

Reflection: In the first chapter of John's Gospel, John the Baptist addresses the reader directly. He explains that he did not baptize Jesus, but the Spirit did. In fact, he did not know Jesus. He was able to recognize him because God, who had sent John the Baptist, had indicated that the man on whom John would see the Spirit descend and remain would be the one who would baptize with the Holy Spirit. John witnessed this and declares to the reader that Jesus is the Son of God. In the Synoptic Gospels (Mark, Matthew, and Luke), the descent of the Spirit occurs as a part of Jesus' baptism (Mark 1:9–11, Matt 3:13–17, Luke 3:21–22).

Naming Jesus Son of God does not indicate his divinity. The author of John's Gospel had indicated that he was God from the opening line (John 1:1). Identifying Jesus as Son of God means that he was chosen for a specific mission. The singer of Psalm 2, usually identified as a royal psalm, one used during the coronation ceremony of Judean kings, states, "I will tell of the decree of the LORD: He said to me, 'You are my son; today I have begotten you'" (Ps 2:7). The day of the new king's coronation is his new birth as a son of God. In other words, God adopts the new king as his son on the day of his enthronement. This is exactly what the author of John's Gospel has in mind. Just as the son-of-God king becomes the earthly agent of God's reign on his coronation day, the son-of-God Jesus becomes the earthly agent of God's kingdom on his baptism day. What is different for Jesus, according to John's Gospel, is that he is both preexistent and incarnate (birth and baptism).

It is very difficult for modern people to grasp the underlying meaning of the name Son of God. In light of the psalmist's understanding, every Judean king was declared to be a son of God on his coronation day. Thus, there were many sons of God throughout Judah's history. The author of John's Gospel applies this understanding to the preexistent Jesus, who is already Son of God at his birth and is revealed by John to be Son of God by his witness of Jesus' baptism with the Holy Spirit. In turn, John reveals what he has seen to the reader.

Journal/Meditation: What new understanding do you have of the name Son of God for Jesus? What deeper truth have you discovered?

Prayer: Son of God, John the Baptist testified that he saw the Spirit descending from heaven like a dove upon you, and it remained on you. Your Father revealed to him that you were the one chosen to baptize with the Holy Spirit. Open the heavens and pour out the

Spirit upon me that I may give witness to you and the Father and the Holy Spirit now and forever and ever. Amen.

Shepherd and Guardian of Souls

Scripture: "When [Christ] was abused, he did not return abuse; when he suffered, he did not threaten; but he entrusted himself to the one who judges justly. He himself bore our sins in his body on the cross, so that, free from sins, we might live for righteousness; by his wounds you [, slaves,] have been healed. For you were going astray like sheep, but now you have returned to the shepherd and guardian of your souls." (1 Pet 2:25)

Reflection: The title of this entry used to be translated in some Bibles as Shepherd and Bishop of Souls. Because the word bishop often carries with it the image of man with a pointed hat (miter) holding a stick (crosier)—which is not what the phrase is attempting to communicate—it is better translated as Shepherd and Guardian of Souls. Furthermore, in the section of the First Letter of Peter from which the above passage comes, the addressees are slaves, who are exhorted by the writer to accept and obey the authority of their masters even if it means suffering. The example of how to do this is Christ, who did not seek revenge, but bore sins to the cross in order that all—slave and free—might live in righteousness. The letter writer's main point is that wounded slaves have been healed by Christ's wounds. The Shepherd and Guardian of their souls has rescued them.

Knowing that the kings of Israel and Judah were considered shepherds may help to understand the role of the guardian. The prophet Jeremiah pronounces woes on the shepherds who destroy and scatter the flock (Jer 23:1–4). As he does in Ezekiel (Ezek 34:1–10), the LORD promises to take over the role of shepherd once the Davidic monarchy becomes extinct. Psalm 23 illustrates this, beginning, "The LORD is my shepherd, I shall not want" (Ps

23:1). In John's Gospel in the Christian Bible (New Testament), Jesus assumes this responsibility (John 10:11, 14).

The Shepherd and Guardian of Souls title for Jesus should bring comfort to us. While slavery in the ancient world was common, in our world it has no place. Nevertheless, the author's point about honorable behavior can be applied to all people. We belong to a flock, whose shepherd is Jesus. Like a good shepherd, he guards us, the flock. However, a shepherd needs honorable sheep. In other words, sheep have to want to be shepherded. The shepherd's staff was a multipurpose tool. It was used to prod sheep forward; it was used to beat back predators; its crook could be used both the pull sheep back into the fold and to pull predators away from the sheep. The sheep would feel safe with a guardian shepherd who genuinely cared for them. Naming Jesus the Shepherd and Guardian of Souls should bring comfort to those who do so.

Journal/Meditation: What images do you associate with the names Shepherd and Guardian? How is Jesus a shepherd for you? How is he a guardian for you?

Prayer: Shepherd and Guardian of Souls, when you were abused, you did not return abuse; when you suffered, you did not threaten. You entrusted yourself to the Father, who judges justly. You bore my sins in your body on the cross, so that, free from sins, I might live for righteousness; by your wounds, I have been healed. For this great gift I praise you now and forever. Amen.

Messiah

Scripture: "One of the two who heard John [the Baptist] speak and followed [Jesus] was Andrew, Simon Peter's brother. He first found his brother Simon and said to him, 'We have found the Messiah' (which is translated Anointed)." (John 1:40–41)

Reflection: Two disciples of John the Baptist, one unnamed and the other Andrew, take the advice of John and without being called follow Jesus. Then, John the Baptist disappears from the scene. Andrew leaves to go and get his brother, Simon Peter, and bring him to Jesus. This unique narrative begins a theme of the Fourth Gospel. Those who come to Jesus often leave, go get others and bring them to him, and then get out of the way. Shortly after this scene Philip imitates Andrew by going to get Nathanael and bringing him to Jesus (John 1:43–51).

Andrew tells his brother, Peter, that he and the other unnamed disciple have found the Messiah. The narrator suddenly interrupts the story with a parenthetical remark directed to the reader about the meaning of the name Messiah. This Hebrew word means anointed. Its Greek equivalent is Christ. Messiah (Christ) is not a Christian Bible (New Testament) name for Jesus; it is a description of his role as the various writers of the Christian Bible (New Testament) first understood it. He is an anointed one, that is, a person chosen by God for a specific mission in the world. The prophet Isaiah applies the description to Cyrus, King of Persia, who defeated the Babylonians and decreed that the Jews in captivity could return to Jerusalem (Isa 44:28, 45:1). Thus, if a foreign ruler could be one of God's anointed ones, Jesus could be, too.

According to the Synoptic Gospels (Mark, Matthew, and Luke), the function of the Messiah was to announce the kingdom of God. According to John's Gospel, the function of the Christ was to perform signs that people might see and believe in the God Jesus was in his incarnate form. According to Paul, the function of the Anointed One was to be a new Adam, one who maintained his trust in God through death and was justified by God through resurrection. Thus, each Christian Bible (New Testament) book presupposes a function that the Messiah is to fulfill. While the name does not indicate divinity, it does lead to multiple understandings of the purpose of the Messiah (Christ, Anointed One).

Journal/Meditation: When you think of Jesus as the Messiah, what meaning do you presuppose for the word Messiah? How can a plurality of meanings, discovered by reading the books of the Christian Bible (New Testament), enrich your understanding?

Prayer: Messiah, Anointed One, God chose you to be the herald of his kingdom, to present signs of the Father's works, and to be the model of righteousness. Like Andrew, I tell others of your presence that I may bring them to you, who live and reign with the Father and the Holy Spirit, one God, forever and ever. Amen.

Savior

Scripture: "[False prophets] promise . . . freedom, but they themselves are slaves of corruption; for people are slaves to whatever masters them. For if, after they have escaped the defilements of the world through the knowledge of our Lord and Savior Jesus Christ, they are again entangled in them and overpowered, the last state has become worse for them than the first." (2 Pet 2:19–20)

Reflection: The author of the Second Letter of Peter provides verse after verse of name-calling those he considers to be false teachers. Such false prophets promise freedom from fear of God's judgment, but such freedom leads those who follow them into the very corruption they had once escaped through their knowledge of the Lord and Savior Jesus Christ. False teachers offer people a way of life without moral integrity, according to the author of this letter; it looks like freedom, but in reality it is slavery. The only way to achieve true freedom is through knowledge of the Lord and Savior, Jesus Christ.

Naming Jesus Savior carries a number of referents in the ancient world. Civic benefactors, people who had wealth and used it to fund buildings and monuments, were often called saviors. Those who were able to help others escape danger were often named saviors. Roman emperors were often called saviors. When the Second Letter of Peter refers to Jesus as Savior, it is stepping into political waters; giving Jesus this title implies that there is one who is greater than civic benefactors and emperors. Jesus rescues people from God's judgment; he saves the godly from trials, while the unrighteous punish themselves as slaves of corruption. Knowledge of the Lord and Savior Jesus Christ enables believers to escape the world's corruption.

What the author of this letter is trying to get at is that there is a true freedom that does not state that one is free to do whatever he or she chooses. This different type of freedom emerges from commitment to Jesus Christ according to the author of Second Peter. While the author does not mention it, this is the freedom that committed, married couples enjoy. This is the freedom that life-time friendships enjoy. This is the freedom that a person who knows himself or herself both inside and outside and is committed to being the best version of himself or herself enjoys. It is not the freedom to do whatever one wants when one wants to do it; it is the freedom to be who God created one to be. Naming Jesus Savior identifies him as the one who taught and lived that type of freedom.

Journal/Meditation: From what or whom do you need to be saved? In what specific ways have you experienced the freedom that the author of the Second Letter of Peter writes about?

Prayer: Savior, with your knowledge of God you rescued people from slavery to corrupted freedom and promised them true freedom as children of God. Grant me the grace always to live in that freedom and not be entangled in the defilements of the world. You live and reign in the freedom of the Father and the Holy Spirit, one God, forever and ever. Amen.

(Chief) Cornerstone

Scripture: ". . . [Y]ou are no longer strangers and aliens, but you are citizens with the saints and also members of the household of God, built upon the foundation of the apostles and prophets, with

Christ Jesus himself as the cornerstone. In him the whole structure is joined together and grows into a holy temple in the Lord." (Eph 2:19–21)

Reflection: The Greek word translated as cornerstone in the above passage can also be translated as keystone. A cornerstone is a stone at the corner of two walls that holds them together; it is a main part of the foundation upon which the building rests. A keystone is the middle stone at the top of an arch; it holds in place the other stones that form the arch. In either case, the operative metaphor employed by the writer of the Letter to the Ephesians is building, specifically a temple. The image may come from the prophet Isaiah, who records the LORD God declaring, "See, I am laying in Zion a foundation stone, a tested stone, a precious cornerstone, a sure foundation" (Isa 28:16). Likewise, Psalm 118, a hymn of thanksgiving, declares, "The stone that the builders rejected has become the chief cornerstone" (Ps 118:22). Both of these verses are quoted by the author of the Second Letter of Peter (2:6–7) when he refers to Jesus as a living stone (2 Pet 2:4).

Paul's usual metaphor for the assembly of believers is body of Christ (Rom 8:10, 12:5; 1 Cor 6:15, 10:16, 12:12, 27; 2 Cor 5:10, 12:2; Gal 2:20; 1 Thess 5:23). While body of Christ is hinted at in Ephesians 3:6 and 5:23 and mentioned in Ephesians 4:12, the operative metaphor is construction and explains why this letter is considered a second-generation Pauline creation.

In the gospels, Jesus refers to himself as the (Chief) Cornerstone (Mark 12:10, Matt 21:42, Luke 20:17), as does the author of the Second Letter of Peter. After telling the parable of the vineyard, an image for the nation of Israel in the Synoptic Gospels, Jesus identifies himself as the stone rejected by the Jews that has become the cornerstone of something new. Likewise, in one of his speeches in the Acts of the Apostles, Peter identifies Jesus as the cornerstone (Acts 4:11). Thus, naming Jesus the (Chief) Cornerstone implies that the foundation of the apostles and prophets, with Christ Jesus himself as the cornerstone, forms a holy temple in which God dwells.

Journal/Meditation: What other implications might there be for naming Jesus the (chief) cornerstone? What other implications might there be for naming him the keystone?

Prayer: Chief Cornerstone, you were rejected like an unfit building stone, but God made you the cornerstone of his new temple. With the grace of the Holy Spirit continue to join together people around the world that, built upon the foundation of the apostles and prophets, all may form a holy temple which echoes with praise for you, the Father, and the Holy Spirit now and forever and ever. Amen.

King of Kings

Scripture: ". . . I [, John of Patmos,] saw heaven opened, and there was a white horse! Its rider is called Faithful and True, and in righteousness he judges and makes war. His eyes are like a flame of fire, and on his head are many diadems; and he has a name inscribed that no one knows but himself. He is clothed in a robe dipped in blood, and his name is called The Word of God. On his robe and on his thigh he has a name inscribed, 'King of kings . . . .'" (Rev 19:11–13, 16)

Reflection: In the Book of Revelation's description of the heavenly warrior, who leads his army to victory over all that is evil, there are four titles or names used to describe him. He is Faithful, that is, he is the bearer of unwavering belief. He is True, that is, he is the witness whose testimony never falls short of the facts. He is the Word of God, that is, he is the All-powerful One's word in human form. And he is King of Kings, that is, he is God (2 Macc 13:4), the blessed and only Sovereign (1 Tim 6:15). His many diadems or crowns indicate that he possesses a royalty beyond any earthly ruler.

John of Patmos's vision of an open door means that the top level of the universe where God lives is open to the middle level of the universe where people live. The warrior on the white horse, the sign of victory, means that he is going to wage a war on evil that he knows he will win. His fiery eyes indicate that he possesses divine knowledge. And like God in the Hebrew Bible (Old Testament), he has a name that no one can know except the Father (Luke 10:22). The blood on his robe indicates his warrior status and the fact that he is ready to tread the wine press of God's wrath (Isa 63:2–3; Rev. 14:19, 19:15). Both on his cloak and seemingly tattooed on his thigh is inscribed King of Kings. The name embroidered on his cloak is a sigil, which identifies the rider on the white horse as Jesus Christ. The same name tattooed on his thigh further describes him as one who has the absolute power of generation and indicates an intimate and solemn oath (Gen 24:2, 24:9, 47:29) to defeat all evil with the Word of God.

Naming Jesus, the Lamb on the throne, King of Kings (Rev 17:14) serves to identify the absolute of the absolute! He trumps anyone who lays claim to the title of king. Since kings are mostly figureheads and tourist attractions today, a modern name might be President of Presidents or Prime Minister of Prime Ministers. In John of Patmos's world, naming the heavenly warrior King of Kings served to challenge the claim of the emperor. Likewise, naming Jesus President of Presidents or Prime Minister of Prime Ministers would serve to challenge human power in the midst of divine rule.

Journal/Meditation: How does naming Jesus King of Kings challenge your human power? In other words, if you think of yourself as Parent of Parents, or Mother of Mothers, or Father of Fathers, what does Jesus' absolute power say to you?

Prayer: King of Kings, on your white horse you are Faithful, True, and the Word of God. Possessing all knowledge, I ask you to judge me in righteousness. Grant that I may one day eternally praise you, who live and reign with the Father and the Holy Spirit, one God, forever and ever. Amen.

Lord of Lords

Scripture: ". . . [T]he armies of heaven, wearing fine line, white and pure, were following [the rider] on white horses. From his mouth comes a sharp sword with which to strike down the nations, and he will rule them with a rod of iron; he will tread the wine press of the fury of the wrath of God. On his robe and on his thigh he has a name inscribed, . . . Lord of lords." (Rev 19:14–16)

Reflection: The heavenly warrior is a commander of the heavenly armies, whose fighters, like him, wear white and ride white horses to indicate the victory they will achieve by conquering evil. The sharp sword that emerges from his mouth is the Word of God, the third name given to him in the previous narrative (Rev 19:13); it is the prophetic word of judgment already mentioned two times in the Book of Revelation (1:16, 2:12). As a servant of God, the Holy One made the warrior's mouth like a sharp sword (Isa 49:2), living and active (Heb 4:12). Once judgment is completed by treading all evil, that is, squeezing all life out of God's enemies, in God's wine press (Rev 14:10, 19), he rules or shepherds all that is good not with a rod of impermanent wood, but with one of permanent iron (Rev 2:27, 12:5).

Both embroidered on his cloak and seemingly tattooed on his thigh is inscribed Lord of Lords. The name embroidered on his cloak is a sigil, which identifies the rider on the white horse as God. In the Book of Deuteronomy, the LORD, Israel's God, is named the Lord of Lords (Deut 10:17), whose steadfast love endures forever (Ps 136:3). In the Book of Daniel, King Nebuchadnezzar of Babylon declares Daniel's God to be the "God of gods and Lord of kings" (Dan 2:47). As stated above, the same name tattooed on his thigh further describes him as one who has the absolute power of generation and indicates an intimate and solemn oath (Gen 24:2, 24:9, 47:29) to defeat all evil with the Word of God.

Like the word *king*, the word *lord* seems archaic in a modern democratic world. Even though the author of Revelation identifies the Lamb on the throne, that is, Jesus, as Lord of lords (Rev 17:14) in its desire to attribute to him the power to command, as it had been attributed previously to the God in the Hebrew Bible (Old Testament), in the Christian Bible (New Testament) it also attributes to him the power to dispose of all evil. And in this regard, like that of King of Kings above, Lord of Lords serves as a challenge to the emperor, who held such power when John of Patmos was writing the Book of Revelation.

Journal/Meditation: What might be a modern, appropriate, and equivalent name for Jesus today? Explain how it captures the various meanings found in the Book of Revelation?

Prayer: Lord of lords, you wield the sharp sword of the Word of God to cleanse the world of evil. Then, after treading it in the wine press of the fury of the wrath of God, you shepherd your people with security and stability. Grant that I be numbered among those in your flock. You live and reign with the Father and the Holy Spirit forever and ever. Amen.

Righteous Judge

Scripture: "I [, Paul,] have fought the good fight, I have finished the race, I have kept the faith. From now on there is reserved for me the crown of righteousness, which the Lord, the righteous judge, will give me on that day, and not only to me but also to all who have longed for his appearing." (2 Tim 4:7–8)

Reflection: The Second of Letter of Paul to Timothy is one written in Paul's name by another author long have Paul was dead. It takes Pauline thought and presents it to a later generation of readers. In the above passage, the author declares the Lord Jesus to be a righteous judge. He will be just, giving to others what they deserve when he appears in glory. The second coming of Christ, often referred to as his parousia, is one of the historical Paul's expectations. In the genuine Pauline letters, he expresses the idea that he will be around when it occurs. The same expectation can be found in the gospels, although each writer handles it differently depending upon the time he is writing. The author of the Second Letter of Paul to Timothy continues to hold onto hope that Jesus will one day appear as judge.

He also presents Paul using athletic metaphors of boxing and racing. According to this author, Paul has won the boxing event, the fight; he has also won the race. Just as winners of athletic events were given a laurel-leaf crown, Paul expects to receive a crown of righteousness; he will be rewarded by the Lord for doing the right thing because it was the right thing to do. The crown will be placed on his head when Jesus returns in glory.

Modern images of judges must be checked when reading this passage. A man or woman sitting behind a high bench dressed in a black robe while holding a gavel in his or her hand is not the image being presented here. Neither is the typical picture of the blindfolded lady holding the scales appropriate. And, the concept of revenge, getting what one deserves, must also be eliminated in order to grasp the meaning of naming Jesus Righteous Judge. This name means mercy, that is, no one will get what he or she deserves. God does not sit behind a bench; he does not hold scales in his hand; and he does not get revenge on his enemies. In the person of his Son, Jesus, named Righteous Judge, he bestows his merciful grace on those who serve him faithfully. That is what naming Jesus Righteous Judge is all about.

Journal/Meditation: When you read the words *righteous* and *judge*, what images come to mind? When you read the word *mercy*, what image comes to mind?

Prayer: Righteous Judge, you reserve a crown of righteousness for those who have served you and your Father faithfully. Grant me the grace to fight the good fight, to finish the race, and to keep the faith that I may be counted as a recipient of your mercy when you appear in glory. You live and reign with the Father and the Holy Spirit, one God, forever and ever. Amen.

Light of the World

Scripture: "Again Jesus spoke to [the Pharisees], saying, 'I am the light of the world. Whoever follows me will never walk in darkness but will have the light of life.'" (John 8:12)

Reflection: One of the underlying presuppositions of John's Gospel is dualism. This philosophical theory of two opposing concepts—in the above passage they are light and darkness—also applies to the body-soul dichotomy, the good-evil dichotomy, and the spiritual-physical dichotomy. Thus, the author of John's Gospel presents Jesus as the light of the world and the world as encompassed by darkness. Using one of the I AM sayings in the Fourth Gospel, Jesus declares that he, God, is light, and, in the words of the First Letter of John, in him there is no darkness (1 John 1:5). Likewise, in the narrative about the man born blind, Jesus tells his disciples, "As long as I am in the world, I am the light of the world" (John 9:5) before restoring the man's sight. Thus, it is easy to conclude that the name Light of the World means that Jesus shines light throughout the darkness.

What Johannine literature seems to ignore is the understanding that darkness is just as revelatory as light! There are times when we can see better in the dark than in the light. There are times when a dim light in a room reveals more truth than a bright lamp. We need to consider the candlelight on many restaurant tables around which two or more people enter into conversation. The light of a fireplace—from wood or gas—fosters intimacy between people. While we experience both light and darkness, the truth may lie somewhere in the middle along a continuum. Instead of the dualism presented in John's Gospel, we might look for the truth in the dialogue between light and darkness.

Biblically, God is both light and darkness. The ninth plague narrated in the Book of Exodus explains how the Egyptians were in the darkness while the Hebrews were in light at the same time (Exod 10:21–23). In the Book of Deuteronomy, Moses reminds the Israelites that they heard God's voice out of darkness while

Mount Horeb (Sinai) was burning with fire (Deut 5:23). Even Psalm 18 sings about the LORD, who is covered by thick darkness from which there emerges light (Ps 18:9b, 11–12). However, the author of Psalm 139 addresses the LORD directly, singing: "If I say, 'Surely the darkness shall cover me, and the light around me become night,' even the darkness is not dark to you; the night is as bright as the day, for darkness is as light to you" (Ps 139:11–12). Thus, naming Jesus the Light of the World should be balanced by also naming him the Darkness of the World!

Journal/Meditation: Where in your life experiences do you find the dualism of light and darkness? Where in your life experiences do you find the dialogue of light and darkness?

Prayer: Light of the World, whoever follows you never walks in darkness but has the light of life. Grant me the light of grace to know the truth that exists in between light and darkness. You live with the Father, for whom the dark is as bright as day, and with the Holy Spirit, who comes as fire out of the darkness, one God, forever and ever. Amen.

Head of the Church

Scripture: "God put his power to work in Christ when he raised him from the dead and seated him at his right hand in the heavenly places, far above all rule and authority and power and dominion, and above every name that is named, not only in this age but also in the age to come. And he has put all things under his feet and has made him the head over all things for the church, which is his body, the fullness of him who fills all in all." (Eph 1:20–23).

Reflection: The unknown author of the Letter to the Ephesians—which is attributed to Paul—reinterprets some genuine Pauline concepts for a different audience at a different time in Christian history. Nowhere in the genuine Pauline letters does Paul refer to Christ as head of the church, as the author of Ephesians does. The author of Ephesians also seems to be more focused on Jesus being at God's powerful right hand with all else under his feet, a sign of his victory and his permanent enthronement. In the genuine Pauline letters, the body of Christ has no head; it is composed of every baptized person. All the members are waiting for Christ to return in glory. In other words, the body of Christ is an assembly of equals awaiting the day of the Lord. This is contrasted to concept in Ephesians where the body of equals has now become a hierarchical gathering of non-equals needing a head or leader, and Christ's imminent return has been pushed back into the distant future.

The Letter to the Colossians, another letter attributed to Paul but written by another author long after Paul was dead, also declares that Jesus, the Son of God, "is the image of the invisible God, the firstborn of all creation" (Col 1:15) and that "he is the head of the body, the church; he is the beginning, the firstborn from the dead, so that he might come to have first place in everything" (Col 1:18). The language is similar to that found in Ephesians, and, like Ephesians, it, too, is focused on Christ's resurrection which enthroned him above all while moving his return in glory to the distant future. What Ephesians and Colossians indicate is the rise of an institution known as the church universal with its need for a head or a leader. Authentic Paul could never have foreseen such a day, because he thought that he would still be around when Jesus returned in glory.

Standing almost two thousand years later and knowing about the various types of Christianity can leave us wondering what happened to the genuine Pauline idea of all members of a local church forming an assembly of equals while awaiting Christ's return in glory. If the Christian world has learned anything in its two thousand years of existence, it knows that in order to survive and grow it needs strong leadership from popes, bishops, pastors, presidents, elders, or whatever other name is given to the person responsible for activating a local church. Thus, while Jesus can be named invisible Head of the Church, another man or woman takes his place visibly in order to keep all the members of the body of Christ on the journey.

Journal/Meditation: Do you imagine the church as a hierarchical structure with Christ as the head or as a community of equals? What are the implications for your image?

Prayer: Head of the Church, your Father put his power to work in you when he raised you from the dead and seated you at his right hand, far above all rule and authority and power and dominion, and above every name that is named, not only in this age but also in the age to come. He put all things under your feet and made you the head over all things for the church, your body, the fullness of him who fills all in all. Keep me faithful to those with whom I assemble, and keep all of us faithful to you, Lord Jesus Christ, who with the Father and the Holy Spirit are one God forever and ever. Amen.

Morning Star

Scripture: "It is I, Jesus, who sent my angel to you with this testimony for the churches. I am the root and the descendant of David, the bright morning star." (Rev 22:16)

Reflection: As can be seen in the above passage from the Book of Revelation, Jesus names himself the bright Morning Star. The author of the Book of Revelation found the image in the Hebrew Bible (Old Testament) Book of Numbers. In one of Balaam's oracles, the prophet declares, ". . . [A] star shall come out of Jacob, and a scepter shall rise out of Israel" (Num 24:17b). The star is a metaphor for the Davidic line of kings that emerged from Judah when the last judge, Samuel, anointed David, son of Jesse, as king of Israel. The passage above portrays Jesus declaring that he is the root and the descendant of David. The prophet Isaiah confirms the star's reference to a king when he refers to the fallen ruler of Babylon as a Day Star (Isa 14:12).

While the Day Star is probably a reference to the planet Venus, in the ancient world being the first star seen at dusk and the last one seen at dawn, the reference in the Book of Revelation is to the Morning Star, which is probably the sun. That is how the Easter Proclamation sung during the night before Easter Sunday in Roman Catholic Churches understands it when it declares that the Morning Star which never sets is Christ, who has been raised from the dead.

Before the Copernican revolution and the understanding that what had once been named stars should be thought of as planets, like Venus, ancient people associated the rise of divinely-provided rulers with the stars in the night sky. A new star was thought to appear in the sky to herald the birth of a world ruler or leader. The author of Matthew's Gospel incorporates this idea into his unique story about magi, astrologers, who set out to find the one whose star they have observed at its rising (Matt 2:2). Under Greek and Roman rulers, the Jews hoped for a ruler who would descend from David's line, bear the messianic titles, and be the Morning Star that overthrew the occupation forces and restored self-rule to Israel. While Jesus did not accomplish that feat, the Book of Revelation nevertheless names him the Morning Star.

Journal/Meditation: What emotions do you associate with the sunrise? Do you connect any of those with the birth of Jesus? If you name Jesus the bright morning star, what are the implications of that image?

Prayer: Morning Star, you have sent your angel to your servant John of Patmos with testimony for the churches. He recorded it in writing and has passed it on to me. Grant that I may understand and heed it. You are the root and the descendant of David, the bright morning star, living and reigning with the Father and the Holy Spirit, one God, forever and ever. Amen.

Sun of Righteousness

Scripture: "See, the day is coming, burning like an oven when all the arrogant and all evildoers will be stubble; the day that comes shall burn them up, says the LORD of hosts, so that it will leave them neither root nor branch. But for you who revere my name the sun of righteousness shall rise, with healing in its wings." (Mal 4:1–2a)

Reflection: As the above passage illustrates, solar imagery is often applied to God in the Hebrew Bible (Old Testament). God is named the sun of righteousness. The image is probably borrowed by the prophet from Egyptian worship of the sun god, known as Re or Ra; the sun god was usually depicted with wings, which further explains Malachi's reference above to healing in its wings. Psalm 4 employs this same imagery, albeit in more subtle way: "Let the light of your face shine on us, O LORD!" (Ps 4:6b). And Psalm 84 declares that "the LORD God is a sun" (Ps 84:11a).

In the context of the Book of Malachi, the solar imagery is employed to describe the punishment of the wicked. The burning heat of the sun, compared to the burning heat of an oven, will set afire the arrogant and evildoers like flame turns grain stalks, that is, stubble, to ashes (Mal 4:3) so that neither root nor branch remains. Once evil is eliminated, only the just, those who revere the name of the LORD, will remain. For them, the sun's heat will bring healing. Just like the sun warms those who stand in it on a cold winter's day, the God who bestows his grace and mercy will heal his people.

When the name Sun of Righteousness is transferred from the LORD God to Jesus, the name denotes the day when Christ will return in glory. It will be a day of final judgment. While the author of Matthew's Gospel skips Malachi's solar imagery, he, nevertheless, employs other metaphors to describe Christ's return to judge the living and the dead. Unique to Matthew's narrative are three metaphorical scenes illustrating judgment. Thus, when Jesus returns as judge, he will separate those who are prepared to enter a wedding feast with a burning lamp from those who failed to bring enough oil (Matt 25:1–13); he will separate those who risked use of their talents from those who buried them while the master was on a journey (Matt 25:14–30); and he will be like a king separating sheep (those who served the needy) from goats (those who did not serve the needy) (Matt 25:31–46). The Sun of Righteousness, Jesus Christ, will heal some and scorch others.

Journal/Meditation: Which image of judgment catches your attention: sun, prepared with a burning lamp, risking the use of talents, or serving the needy? What are the implications of your chosen image for yourself?

Prayer: Sun of Righteousness, when you return in glory, the arrogant and all evildoers will become stubble that is burned. Heal me with your grace and mercy that I may be prepared to enter your wedding feast, that I may willingly risk the use of my talents to spread your name, and that I may see you in the needy and praise your name. You are the Lord Jesus Christ forever and ever. Amen.

Lord Jesus (Christ)

Scripture: ". . . Peter stood up and said to [the apostles and elders], 'My brothers, you know that in the early days God made a choice among you, that I should be the one through whom the Gentiles would hear the message of the good news and become believers. And God, who knows the human heart, testified to them by giving them the Holy Spirit, just as he did to us; and in cleansing their hearts by faith he has made no distinction between them and us. . . . [W]e believe that we will be saved through the grace of the Lord Jesus, just as they will." (Acts 15:7–9, 11)

Reflection: The speech given by Peter is part of the proceedings of the assembly of apostles and elders held in Jerusalem to decide about the incorporation of the Gentiles into the body of believers, who had all at first been Jews. The question needing an answer was this: Do Gentile believers have to become Jewish believers first? Peter's astounding answer to that question is No! Up to this point in the Acts of the Apostles, Peter has launched the mission to the Gentiles, a mission which Paul will take over and carry to the ends of the earth. Peter has discovered that God shows no partiality with the Holy Spirit; he pours it on both Jews and Gentiles. And he concludes by declaring that God saves both Jews and Gentiles through the grace of the Lord Jesus, to which some manuscripts add Christ.

In naming the source of salvation to be the Lord Jesus, Peter declares that both Jews and Gentiles are now heirs of God's promises to Israel. The major issue dividing Jews and Gentiles, namely, circumcision—the sign of being incorporated into the covenant God made with Abraham—no longer exists as far as Peter is concerned. Circumcision is not necessary for salvation; what is necessary is the grace of the Lord Jesus (Christ) which God has offered through him to both Jews and Gentiles. The great divide between Jews and Gentiles, caused by circumcision, has been removed. Furthermore, God has demonstrated this by giving the Holy Spirit both to Jews (Acts 2:1–13) and Gentiles (Acts 10:44–48).

Thus, naming Jesus the Lord and Christ identifies him as Master and Anointed. Jesus is the new power and authority (Master) which has been confirmed by God (Anointed) with the manifestation of grace named Holy Spirit. While Peter's radical words have lost much of their shock today, the author of the Acts of the Apostles understands this as a turning point in the spread of what ultimately came to be known as Christianity. Peter recognized that God was doing something new, and even though he probably had no idea where it would lead, his mission was to participate in it by tearing down a wall that divided Jews from Gentiles.

Journal/Meditation: Where do recognize divisions between people today? How can you be like Peter, tearing down the walls that divide?

Prayer: Lord Jesus Christ, for two thousand years believers have spread the message of the good news of God's grace to Jews and Gentiles by pouring on them the Holy Spirit and removing whatever divided them from each other. Renew this grace among people that all may come to recognize that they are brothers and sisters of one God, who lives and reigns as Father, Son, and Holy Spirit, forever and ever. Amen.

Chief Shepherd

Scripture: ". . . I exhort the elders among you to tend the flock of God that is in your charge, exercising the oversight, not under compulsion but willingly, as God would have you do it . . . . And when the chief shepherd appears, you will win the crown of glory that never fades away." (1 Pet 5:1–2, 4)

Reflection: In the above passage from the First Letter of Peter, the author exhorts local shepherds, named elders, to take care of their people by being courageous leaders who have discerned the will of God. In his exhortation, he tells those who lead the community to tend the flock of God, a reference to the Hebrew Bible (Old Testament) idea that God is the shepherd of his people Israel, but now through Jesus elders are to serve as local shepherds. Continuing to use his sheep and shepherd analogy, he promises them that when the chief shepherd, Jesus Christ, appears, they will be given a crown of glory. It is a crown that does not fade or wilt, as do typical laurel crowns given to athletes; this one represents God's approval that awaits those elders, shepherds, who fulfill their responsibilities. In the in-between time, local elders or shepherds recognize that they receive their commission to care for the sheep (people) from Jesus, who received it from God.

Unpacking the meaning of the name Chief Shepherd requires some in-depth reflection on this multi-level analogy of shepherd/ leader. While there are multiple Hebrew Bible (Old Testament) references to God as the shepherd of Israel (Ps 80:1), one of the best is Psalm 23; the opening line states, "The LORD is my shepherd" (Ps 23:1). Psalm 77 explains how God often chooses others through whom he leads his flock, in this case "by the hand of Moses and Aaron" (Ps 77:20). Ultimately, the role of shepherding the flock is passed on to the kings of Israel and Judah, but, as Jeremiah explains, they have not fulfilled their duty. So, the LORD declares that he will raise up new shepherds who will shepherd them (Jer 23:1–4). Ezekiel expresses the same (Ezek 34:1–24, 31).

Assigning the name Chief Shepherd to Jesus means there is a hierarchy of shepherds. On the bottom are the local shepherds of churches and parishes, commonly known as pastors (from the Latin word for shepherd). Coordinating and above them are regional superiors or bishops, who are responsible for shepherding some type of geographical area. Geographical areas within countries may also have a shepherd over all of them. Then, according to the First Letter of Peter, Jesus is the Chief Shepherd, commissioned by the LORD Shepherd, whose arrival in glory is awaited.

Journal/Meditation: What might be a contemporary title for Jesus that captures the essence of the meaning of Chief Shepherd? On what levels do you have shepherds: locally, geographically, nationally, and universally?

Prayer: Chief Shepherd, you never leave the flock of your people unattended. Raise up shepherds filled with the wisdom of the Holy Spirit who can exercise oversight of the flock faithfully and diligently so that when you appear in glory they may receive the crown of eternal life that never fades away. You live and reign with the LORD our shepherd and the Holy Spirit, one God, forever and ever. Amen.

Resurrection and Life

Scripture: "Jesus said to [Martha], 'I am the resurrection and the life. Those who believe in me, even though they die, will live, and everyone who lives and believes in me will never die. Do you be-lieve this?'" (John 11:25-26)

Reflection: Employing one of the typical I AM sayings in John's Gospel, Jesus goes to see Martha and Mary, whose brother, Lazarus, has died, and tells Martha that he is incarnate, eternal life. After a short dialogue with her, she leaves to get her sister, Mary, who, after coming to Jesus, goes with him to the tomb where Lazarus's body has been placed. The Johannine author makes sure that the reader understands that it was a cave with a round stone that sealed the entrance. On a shelf in the cave a dead body was wrapped in linen and laid to rest. After a few years, the cave could be opened, the bones collected and placed in an ossuary (bone box), and the box placed below the shelf which could be used again. Rolling away the stone from the entrance to the cave would permit a stench to emerge to greet those standing nearby. Martha knows this and ex-presses it to Jesus (John 11:39). Again, Jesus must remind Martha that he manifests the glory of God.

In order to demonstrate that he is the resurrection and the life—not to mention the fact that he is God incarnate—the Johan-nine Jesus prays and then calls Lazarus to come out (John 11:43). The dead man emerges to the astonishment of all present. He has been resuscitated, brought back to life. But he serves as a sign of what will happen next to Jesus; he will die, but God will raise him to new life. Furthermore, in John's Gospel a sign is given in order to spark faith in those who see it. And so many who had seen what Jesus did for Lazarus, Martha, and Mary come to believe in him (John 11:45).

Naming Jesus Resurrection and Life means that resurrection and life overlap. The Johannine Jesus is the incarnation of eternal life. This life as we know it is changed; it is not ended. We pass through death in order to be raised to life on the other side. We experience eternal life now, and that should enable us to believe in a smooth transition to its fullness on the other side of death. The experiences of genuine love, of insight, of wisdom, of spirit, of peace, of grace, etc. are glimpses of the fullness that await us eternally. This is the will of Jesus' Father: All should pass through death to resurrected life!

Journal/Meditation: What is your greatest fear concerning your death? How does Jesus calm that fear? How does the account of the raising of Lazarus (John 11:1–45) engender faith in you?

Prayer: Resurrection and Life, those who believe in you, even though they die, will live, and everyone who lives and believes in you will never die. Strengthen this faith within me with daily experiences of eternal life, and grant that I may share it fully with you and the Father and the Holy Spirit forever and ever. Amen.

Horn of Salvation

Scripture: "Blessed be the Lord God of Israel, for he has looked favorable on his people and redeemed them. He has raised up a mighty savior for us in the house of his servant David . . . ." (Luke 1:68–69)

Reflection: The words *mighty savior* represent the Greek words for *horn of salvation*. Older English Bible translations kept horn of salvation, but, because the concept is less understood by modern Bible readers, new translations change it to mighty savior. In the ancient world, a horn was a sign of power. It could be a ram's, goat's, or ox's horn that represented success, victory, or vindication. Throughout the Hebrew Bible (Old Testament) a horn is used to represent strength; a horn also contained the oil used to anoint David and his descendants. That is why the author of Luke's Gospel employs it in the canticle the father of John the Baptist utters (Luke 1:68–79). Zechariah declares that God has raised the power of salvation in his midst and his own son, John the Baptist, will be his prophet (Luke 1:76–77). Jesus, the anointed one, is the Horn of Salvation; he is the mighty savior. His predecessor, John the Baptist, will do the anointing, that is, preparing his way.

As the horn of salvation, the mighty savior, Jesus brought freedom and security to people so they could stand before their God, who preserves life. In the Synoptic Gospels (Mark, Matthew, and Luke), the faith of Jews and Gentiles moves Jesus to declare that they are healed and saved. In John's Gospel, Jesus' signs spark the faith that saves. While Jesus serves as the horn of salvation for anything that interrupts the relationship between God and people, he also saves from sins; he enables people to escape whatever has engulfed them in the world. This is not a static act. It is an ongoing, lifetime process of removing anything that gets in the way of standing before God in freedom and security brought by the Horn of Salvation.

While horns today do not carry the meaning they did for ancient people, modern inhabitants of the world still need freedom and security to stand before their God. Relationship possessiveness or manipulation robs recipients of their freedom. Stock market or any other financial insecurity can paralyze investors. Sometimes just driving to the grocery store or the bank can instill the fear of getting into an accident in the driver of the automobile. Naming Jesus the Horn of Salvation or the Mighty Savior will not remove the daily attacks on freedom and security, but it can remind us that our relationship with God can flourish only when we stand in the freedom and security brought to us by the very same God in the person of his Son, Jesus Christ.

Journal/Meditation: What attacks your freedom and security? How does that affect your relationship with God? What can you do to remove those attacks or lessen their impact on your life?

Prayer: Horn of Salvation, Mighty Savior, you were raised up by God as a sign of his favor to redeem all his people from their enemies and show them mercy. Grant me the grace to serve you without fear and in holiness and righteousness all the days of my life. You live and reign with the Father and the Holy Spirit, one God, forever and ever. Amen.

Governor

Scripture: ". . . [Y]ou, Bethlehem, in the land of Judah, are by no means least among the rulers of Judah; for from you shall come a ruler who is to shepherd my people Israel." (Matt 2:6)

Reflection: The author of Matthew's Gospel loves to quote from the Hebrew Bible (Old Testament); however, most of the time he does not quote accurately. For example, the above quotation comes from the prophet Micah: ". . . [Y]ou, O Bethlehem of Ephrathah, who are one of the little clans of Judah, from you shall come forth for me one who is to rule in Israel, whose origin is from of old, from ancient days" (Mic 5:2). The quotation associates a new ruler over a restored Israel with Bethlehem, David's home town, and with Ephrathah, David's clan. Bethlehem was a very tiny village that produced the great David. In other words, it is a rags to riches story. Micah is announcing that the coming ruler will revive the Davidic dynasty which ruled in Jerusalem before the city fell to the Babylonians in 587 BCE. We know from history that this never occurred. That historical fact, however, does not keep the author of Matthew's Gospel from using it in a unique story about King Herod consulting the chief priests about where a Messiah was to be born before dealing with magi (Matt 2:1–12). The author of Matthew's Gospel presents Jesus' birth in Bethlehem, where Mary and Joseph live, as the fulfillment of Micah's words.

In some older biblical translations the phrase "a ruler who is to shepherd" in Matthew's Gospel is often rendered as "a governor who is to rule." In general, no matter the translation, the oracle leaves open possible interpretations of which Matthew's is one. There even may be some rejection of whoever the current ruler was at the time of the writing of the oracle in favor of a new one. A governor is someone in authority who rules the people in a geographically-defined area, such as a state, a colony, or a province. When Matthew's use of Micah's words are translated with governor and applied to Jesus, the author is presenting him as the

Davidic descendant who emerges from tiny Bethlehem as a great king to rule the world.

Naming Jesus Governor today may be archaic. At least in the United States, the word governor is primarily applied to the highest office in state government. While Jesus is named king in the Roman Catholic liturgical calendar, the name also may be archaic in a country which elects a new president every four years. Ruler, too, probably carries a lot of royal baggage. Leader may be the name with the least amount of negativity associated with it.

Journal/Meditation: What are the connotations of governor, king, ruler, and leader for you? In your opinion, which of those best names Jesus? Why?

Prayer: Governor, whose origin is from of old, from Bethlehem and from one of the little clans of Judah, you came forth to rule and shepherd God's people Israel. As in ancient days, come and rule in my heart and mind. I ask this in your name, Lord Jesus Christ; you live and reign forever and ever. Amen.

Alpha and Omega

Scripture: "'I am the Alpha and the Omega,' says the Lord God, who is and who was and who is to come, the Almighty." (Rev 1:8)

Reflection: In the Book of Revelation, God claims the name Alpha and Omega. Alpha is the first letter of the Greek alphabet, like A is in English. Omega, meaning big (or long) O, is the last letter of the Greek alphabet, like Z is in English. If these words were being written today, the author would say from A to Z. "I am the A and the Z" is to claim absolute power over everything from the mythological presupposed beginning to the mythological presupposed end. The line is repeated by God, identified as the one seated on the throne (Rev 21:5), later in the book: "I am the Alpha and the Omega, the beginning and the end" (Rev 21:6b). However, the line's third occurrence features Jesus, the one coming soon (Rev 22:12), saying, "I am the Alpha and the Omega, the first and the last, the beginning and the end" (Rev 22:13). The name that had been used to identify God is now employed to identify Jesus.

In the world created by the narrative of the Book of Revelation, there is repeated the early Christian hope that Jesus would return soon. He says so in Revelation 22:12: "See, I am coming soon; my reward is with me, to repay according to everyone's work." This hope enabled the first couple of generations of Jesus' followers to endure life while awaiting his return. But as the days turned into years and the years into decades and the decades into centuries, the hope began to wane.

We stand two thousand years later, still waiting while getting on with life—growing up, marrying, conceiving and raising children, pursuing careers and jobs, and looking forward to retirement. No one of us expects to see Jesus return in our own lifetime! What began as an imminent expectation has now been pushed so far into the future that it barely matters to us anymore. Naming Jesus the Alpha and Omega attributes to him the same all-encompassing characteristics of God. It paves the way for a Christian declaration over two hundred years away from the writing of the Book of Revelation that Jesus is one hundred percent man and one hundred percent God.

Journal/Meditation: How have you experienced being all-encompassed by God or Jesus?

Prayer: Alpha and Omega, you are coming soon and bringing your reward with you to repay according to everyone's work. Grant that I may experience the beginning and end of your great love. You are the first and last, living and reigning with the Father and the Holy Spirit, one God, forever and ever. Amen.

Bread of Life

Scripture: Jesus said to [the crowd], "I am the bread of life. Whoever comes to me will never be hungry, and whoever believes in me will never be thirsty." (John 6:35)

Reflection: Using one of the famous I AM statements in John's Gospel, Jesus declares that he is the sustenance for his followers. Those who believe that he came from God and follow him have their spiritual hunger satisfied. Likewise, they have their spiritual thirst quenched. Earlier in the long discourse, the Johannine Jesus tells the members of the crowd that it is his Father who gives them the true bread from heaven (John 6:32), and he is that bread of God which gives life to the world (John 6:33).

These words from the Johannine Jesus are found in the first (John 6:22–40) of three dialogues (John 6:41–49, 6:60–71) following the narrative of the feeding of five thousand people (John 6:10). This story (John 6:2–13) resembles another one found in the Synoptic Gospels (Mark 6:30–44, Matt 14:13–21, Luke 9:10–17), which means that it circulated widely in oral tradition before being written by various Christian Bible (New Testament) authors. In John's Gospel, it features signs. The story begins with five barley loaves and two fish (John 6:9), which, of course, equal the sacred number seven, itself a sum of three (indicating the divine) and four (indicating the earth). In other words, God is being revealed on the earth. Five (John 6:9), representing grace (as in five books of Torah and five major discourses in Matthew's Gospel), is intensified by multiplying it by a thousand to signify immensity; five thousand are fed (John 6:10). After everyone has eaten, twelve baskets of leftovers are gathered (John 6:13); twelve represents the tribes of Israel and the new people of God. In sign language, the narrator is declaring that God sustains his people through Jesus, just as he once did in the desert through Moses (John 6:32).

While the focus of the narrative is on eating bread and drinking wine, that is, eating Jesus the living bread of life (John 6:48, 51) and drinking his blood (John 6:53–56), there is more depth to the words than may at first appear. Those who eat living bread will live eternally. Those who drink blood drink life that is sacred to God and are transfused with eternal life. Some in the narrative understand Jesus' words literally, while those reading them may begin to notice that there are multiple ways to eat living bread and drink living blood without ever eating or drinking anything. This deeper truth often not verbalized is experienced when families gather around a table and pass around food on Thanksgiving, Christmas, and Easter; when husbands and wives renew themselves in the quiet corner of a restaurant; and when friends share what really matters in their lives. Jesus, who is manifest in every person, gives himself to another as the Bread of Life.

Journal/Meditation: When and specifically how have you experienced Jesus as the Bread of Life other than when celebrating the Lord's Supper?

Prayer: Bread of Life, you were sent from heaven by your Father to be the bread that gives life to the world. Feed me with this bread throughout my life so that I do not hunger, and grant that I may one day share in eternal life with you, the Father, and the Holy Spirit, one God, forever and ever. Amen.

Rabbi

Scripture: "When Jesus turned and saw [two of John the Baptist's disciples] following [him], he said to them, 'What are you looking for?' They said to him, 'Rabbi' (which translated means Teacher), 'where are you staying?' He said to them, 'Come and see.' They came and saw where he was staying, and they remained with him that day." (John 1:38–39ab)

Reflection: The author of John's Gospel likes to translate words for the readers when he uses what may have been unfamiliar words for them. For example, in the passage above, he explains that the word *Rabbi* means *Teacher.* He does this because at the time of Jesus the word *rabbi* meant *master* or *my master.* It is only in later Jewish history that the name *rabbi* becomes a title for Jesus instead of a form of address as illustrated above. Because it can also mean *my great one,* as a title it treats the one addressed as someone deserving respect and not as a theologian authorized to teach theology. The author of this gospel uses this title for Jesus a total of eight times (John 1:49; 3:2, 26; 4:31; 6:25; 9:2, and 11:8) to indicate Jesus' perfection. While it is also used in Mark's Gospel (9:5; 11:21; 14:45) and Matthew's Gospel (23:7, 8; 26:25, 49), in John's Gospel it takes on special significance through its usage.

The author of the Fourth Gospel also employs the title *Rabbouni,* and again he explains that it means *Teacher* (John 20:16). Rabbouni may be an emphatic form of rabbi, or it may reflect the way the word *rabbi* was pronounced at the time of Jesus. The word occurs in only one other place in the Christian Bible (New Testament); that is Mark's Gospel (10:51), where it is presented in many Bibles as *my teacher* instead of rabbouni.

While the word *rabbi* or *rabbouni* is used for Jesus in the Christian Bible (New Testament), it is seldom used by the general public today. If it were, it may serve to connote Jesus' Jewish origin, since Jewish leaders are usually called rabbi. Otherwise, today's modern equivalent would probably be Mister, Teacher, Doctor, or Professor. Those are the ways we address those we think deserve respect. Naming Jesus Rabbi or Rabbouni designated the same in the ancient world.

Journal/Meditation: For you what would a name be for Jesus that designates respect? Explain.

Prayer: Rabbi, you invited two of John's disciples to come and see where you were staying. I, too, hear you invitation and readily respond by remaining in your presence all day. Grant that one day I may see you face to face for all eternity. You are the Teacher, living and reigning with the Father and the Holy Spirit, one God, forever and ever. Amen.

59

Firstborn

Scripture: "We know that all things work together for good for those who love God, who are called according to his purpose. For those whom he foreknew he also predestined to be conformed to the image of his Son, in order that he might be the firstborn within a large family." (Rom 8:28–29)

Reflection: According to Paul in his letter to the Romans, God has a greater purpose that has now been revealed. God works for the greater good through all things, and so people are called to become a part of the Holy One's plan to save them. There is no time in God—or all time past, present, and future exists in him; we are not able even to conceive of all time existing at once, so Paul states that God predestined all to be shaped into the image of his Son. This makes the Son the firstborn of the LORD's new family of those who have been raised from the dead. In his First Letter to the Corinthians, Paul refers to Christ as "the first fruits of those who have died" (1 Cor 15:23).

This same idea is found in the Book of Revelation. There, Jesus Christ is called "the firstborn of the dead" (Rev 1:5). What the author means is that Jesus is the first person to have died and been raised to new life by God. The Letter to the Hebrews uses the word *firstborn* to refer to Jesus' birth (Heb 1:6), but, like Revelation, it also refers to "the firstborn who are enrolled in heaven" (Heb 12:23). So, the word *firstborn* can refer to the person born first in a family, and it can refer to the firstborn from the dead, both Jesus and those who have followed him.

It is not uncommon to hear people talk about their long-range plans. In order for a two- to three-week trip to take place, a plan must be formulated in advance in order to get ready. A checklist is made, and as a date is set, airline tickets are purchased, and the pets are entrusted to someone's care, the plan gradually reaches fulfillment. Daily plans follow the same outline. There is a final time when one must get out of bed, shower, and head to work or wherever else one needs to go. Without the plan, several (to many) things can cause chaos that disrupts the rest of the day. Paul's insight about Jesus being the firstborn enabled him to write about God's plan as he understood it in the middle of the first Christian century. Naming Jesus Firstborn acknowledges God's timeless plan.

Journal/Meditation: What is your next long-range plan? What items are on your checklist? What role does God play in your plan?

Prayer: Firstborn, your birth brought great rejoicing for the whole world, but your resurrection from the dead revealed how your Father makes all things work together for those who love him, for those he calls according to his purpose. Conform me to your image that I may one day join your family in the kingdom where you live and reign forever and ever. Amen.

Gate

Scripture: ". . . Jesus said to [the Pharisees], 'Very truly, I tell you, I am the gate for the sheep. I am the gate. Whoever enters by me will be saved, and will come in and go out and find pasture.'" (John 10:7, 9)

Reflection: Older biblical translations often refer to Jesus as the door for the sheep. However, modern translations, keeping with the operative metaphor of shepherd, prefer to use the word *gate*. Instead of introducing a word that carries a different connotation, gate maintains the imagery of a shepherd herding his sheep into a stone enclosure—called a sheepfold (John 10:1)—through a gate, which can be shut to keep the sheep within the pen. In the morning the shepherd opens the gate and leads the flock to pasture (John 10:2–3).

Presenting another one of the standard I AM sayings found in John's Gospel, Jesus extends the sheep and shepherd metaphor by claiming that he (God) is the gate, a movable barrier that opens and closes a gap in a fence or wall. What this means is that Jesus himself is the one who provides access to God, the source of salvation. One can join the community of sheep only by going through the gate, Jesus, to God.

Naming Jesus Gate reveals strong biblical truth. In the Bible, both God and human rulers are often referred to as shepherds of the sheep (people). However, while God remains faithful, rulers get caught up in politics and fail to care for the sheep. In claiming himself as the gate, the Johannine Jesus reveals himself as the point of access both to the community of believers and God his Father. Those who belong to the sheep both enter the sheepfold through Jesus for protection and access to God and leave it through him for access to pasture—food and water. As the good shepherd, he lays down his life for them.

Journal/Meditation: Because the operative metaphor of sheep, shepherd, sheepfold, and gate is not readily accessible for most people, what equivalent metaphor can you think of that captures the same concept for modern people?

Prayer: Gate, you provide salvation to all who follow you. You are access to God. Keep me from straying. Repeatedly call me into the divine presence through you that I may enjoy the kingdom where you, Jesus Christ, live with the Father and the Holy Spirit, one God, forever and ever. Amen.

Faithful Witness

Scripture: "John to the seven churches that are in Asia: Grace to you and peace from him who is and who was and who is to come, and from the seven spirits who are before his throne, and from Jesus Christ, the faithful witness, the firstborn of the dead, and the rulers of the kings of the earth." (Rev 1:4–5a)

Reflection: In the Book of Revelation, the above passage introduces the letter-writing genre of the work (Rev 2:1–3:22). Using a standard ancient beginning, John of Patmos—the pseudonymous mediator between Jesus Christ and the seven specified churches in Asia—wishes grace to the recipients of the letters. Grace, God's offer of himself to people, is presented as having three sources. The first is the Father, the one who is and who was and was to come. The second is the Holy Spirit, identified as seven spirits—perfect and complete—before the divine throne. And third is Jesus, who is identified with three names: faithful witness, firstborn of the dead, and ruler of the kings of the earth. Being the firstborn from the dead refers to his resurrection, and ruler of the kings of the earth refers to his reign. What concerns us here is the name Faithful Witness.

Faithful Witness refers to Jesus' death. The Greek word for witness yields another word in English: martyr. When the Book of Revelation names Jesus the Faithful Witness, it means that he committed his life to truth, even suffering death on behalf of the truth. In the letter to the church in Laodicea, he is called the "faithful and true witness" (Rev 3:14). While our modern understanding of witness—as one who tells the truth about what was seen, heard, or known—stems from the role one plays in a court of law, the Faithful Witness of the Book of Revelation carries with it the added connotation that it cost the witness his life; he was martyred for his faithful witness.

Around the world every year there are countless faithful witnesses who not only attest to truth, but often give their lives because of it. Those who point out prejudice based on skin color, sex, or creed may find themselves dead. Those who remain true to the principles of their faith may discover persecution that leads to death. Sometimes just being in the right place at the wrong time results in faithful witness to death. The name Faithful Witness applied to Jesus indicates his commitment to truth all the way to death on the cross.

Journal/Meditation: In what specific ways are you a faithful witness?

Prayer: Faithful Witness, you remained committed to the truth even though it made you a martyr on the cross. Fill me with the grace of the Father and the Holy Spirit that I may bear faithful witness to the triune God forever and ever. Amen.

Son of the Most High

Scripture: "The angel said to her, 'Do not be afraid, Mary, for you have found favor with God. And now, you will conceive in your womb and bear a son, and you will name him Jesus. He will be great and will be called the Son of the Most High, and the Lord God will give to him the throne of his ancestor David.'" (Luke 1:30–32)

Reflection: The angel Gabriel's words to Mary name Jesus as Son of the Most High. Most High is another way to name God, even as he is referred to a few words later as Lord God. The author of Matthew's Gospel prefers to name Jesus Son of God (Matt 2:15; 3:17; 4:3, 6), while the author of John's Gospel prefers the Only Son of God (John 1:18) and Mark's Gospel uses Son of the Blessed One (Mark 14:61), still another way to name God.

The word Son implies a Father-Son metaphor. This should not strike us as unusual considering that the Bible came out of a patriarchal culture in which "Sons are indeed a heritage from the LORD" (Ps 127:3). When God is referred to as Father, the same metaphor is being employed, as a man is not a father until he procreates a son or daughter. The birth of his son or daughter bestows upon him the title of father. When Jesus is referred to as Son of the Most High, Son of God, or Son of the Blessed One, the patriarchal metaphor enables us to talk about Jesus' relationship to God in human language. However, such language is never adequate; it must be clarified with the understanding that the Son of God was always being begotten by God. There was never a time when he was not. Metaphors always capture some of the truth while also not capturing all of the truth. This is because no one thing is exactly like another thing. A metaphor is an implicit comparison; it is figurative and cannot literally capture the total truth of the reality it is attempting to identify. If the Bible had grown up in a matriarchal culture, the metaphor might be the Daughter-Mother relationship or the Niece-Aunt relationship. Today, we must search for metaphors that speak to modern people who do not live in a patriarchal culture. In other words, there are other ways to speak of the relationship that Jesus has with God other than Son of the Most High.

Journal/Meditation: What other metaphors can you use for the Jesus-God relationship? What truth does each disclose? What truth does each not capture?

Prayer: Son of the Most High, the angel Gabriel announced to Mary of Nazareth that she had found so much favor with God that she would conceive you in her womb. The angel told her that you would be great and inherit the throne of your ancestor David. Grant me a share of Mary's grace that I may one day join her in praising you forever and ever. Amen.

Great High Priest

Scripture: "Since, then, we have a great high priest who has passed through the heavens, Jesus, the Son of God, let us hold fast to our confession. For we do not have a high priest who is unable to sympathize with our weaknesses, but we have one who in every respect has been tested as we are, yet without sin." (Heb 4:14–15).

Reflection: The anonymous author of the misnamed Letter to the Hebrews refers to Jesus as a Great High Priest. The document, which seems to be an exhortation and argument in a vague letter form, also refers to Jesus as the High Priest (Heb 3:1; 6:20) and Faithful High Priest (Heb 2:17). The common word in all these names is priest; the origin of the hereditary Hebrew Bible (Old Testament) priesthood begins with Aaron and then Levi. By the time of Jesus and the writing of Hebrews, the high priest was the most important person. He was head of the Temple cult, president of the Sanhedrin, and the chief representative of the people to the ruling officers of foreign powers that controlled Jerusalem and its environs.

When the author of Hebrews names Jesus Great High Priest, he is declaring that Jesus replaces the office with himself. He not only makes the offering to God, but he is the offering he offers to God. What was once enacted on earth is now enacted in heaven states Hebrews. Jesus is the perfect atonement because he is God's Son. His once-for-all offering of himself abolishes all the animal sacrifices of the past and brings redemption, salvation, forgiveness, purification, sanctification, and perfection. Thus, Jesus is the founder of a new cult.

Naming Jesus Great High Priest carries several connotations. The word great places him in a position above all previous Jewish high priests; he replaces even Aaron, Levi, and their descendants. As a high priest, he functions in a once-for-all capacity, effectively abolishing all priesthood that went before him. Furthermore, not being descended from a high priestly family, there is a newness to the role claimed for him by the author of the Letter to the Hebrews. He is a priest, one who offers sacrifice; however, he offers the best sacrifice—himself—to God. He was able to identify with us because of his humanity, but because of his status as Son he has passed into the heavens.

Journal/Meditation: How does Jesus function as a Great High Priest for you?

Prayer: Great High Priest, you offered yourself in sacrifice for the sins of the world and passed through the heavens to God. Grant me the grace to hold fast to my confession even as you sympathize with my human weakness. You live and reign with the Father and the Holy Spirit, Lord Jesus Christ, forever and ever. Amen.

Adam

Scripture: "'The first man, Adam, became a living being'; the last Adam became a life-giving spirit." (1 Cor 15:45)

Reflection: In his First Letter to the Corinthians, Paul contrasts the first Adam and the last Adam. The first Adam is the man in Genesis 2:7 into whom the LORD God breathed the breath of life, making the man a living being. The last Adam, Jesus, gives the breath of life-giving spirit. Paul also refers to this contrast in his Letter to the Romans in which he declares the first Adam to be "a type of the one who was to come" (Rom 5:14).

The first Adam represents the origin of sin and death for Paul. The last Adam represents the free gift of grace. According to Paul, God decided to start over. The result of the first Adam's disobedience was God's condemnation; the result of the last Adam's obedience is justification. People are recreated in grace and righteousness through God's work in the last Adam, Jesus Christ. "Therefore just as one man's trespass led to condemnation for all, so one man's act of righteousness leads to justification and life for all," states Paul (Rom 5:18). He adds, "For just as by the one man's disobedience the many were made sinners, so by the one man's obedience the many will be made righteous" (Rom 5:19).

In naming Jesus Adam, a name meaning *man*, Paul identifies him as a living being. Because God raised Christ from the dead, Paul also identifies him as a life-giving spirit. What the first Adam messed up for all in terms of relationship with God, the last Adam straightened out in terms of relationship with God. Paul understands Jesus to be the new man God created in order to show people how to live in God's life-giving grace and spirit. Thus, naming Jesus Adam implies that a new and better model of who people can be in cooperation with God has been given.

Journal/Meditation: What other implications are there to naming Jesus the last Adam? How is Jesus a model of living in a cooperative relationship with God for you?

Prayer: Adam, through your resurrection from the dead, you became a life-giving spirit for all those who were merely living beings. Where sin once abounded, grace has abounded even more. Fill me with your gracious, life-giving spirit that I may serve you now and in the life to come. You live and reign with the Father and the Holy Spirit, one God, forever and ever. Amen.

Bridegroom

Scripture: John the Baptist said: "He who has the bride is the bridegroom. The friend of the bridegroom, who stands and hears him, rejoices greatly at the bridegroom's voice. For this reason my joy has been fulfilled. He must increase, but I must decrease." (John 3:29–30)

Reflection: Bridegroom imagery is common in the Hebrew Bible (Old Testament). The prophet Isaiah presents God as the bridegroom who rejoices over the bride, his people (Isa 62:5), as does the prophet Jeremiah (2:2). The prophet Hosea applies the metaphor to God as husband and his people the bride (Hos 2:16–20). This imagery spills into the Christian Bible (New Testament) as seen in the passage above. The author of John's Gospel portrays John the Baptist declaring that the bridegroom, Jesus, has the bride, believers. John's role is best man; he keeps the bridegroom center stage; he decreases in importance while the bridegroom increases in importance.

The author of Mark's Gospel portrays Jesus comparing himself to the bridegroom at a wedding. No one fasts during a wedding, which was taking place between Jesus and people. However, when the bridegroom leaves, that is, dies and is raised, then people will fast (Mark 2:19–20). The Gospel of Matthew copies the same idea from Mark (Matt 9:14–15) as does the author of Luke's Gospel (5:33–35). Matthew's Gospel contains an allegory of ten bridesmaids going out to meet the bridegroom; five of the bridesmaids were foolish and five were wise (Matt 25:1–12). The bridegroom is Jesus, who has returned to celebrate with those five wise bridesmaids who have earned a place in the banquet hall by living righteous lives. The Book of Revelation proclaims the "the marriage of the Lamb has come, and his bride has made herself ready" (Rev 19:7b), and later describes the new Jerusalem coming down out of heaven to be "prepared as a bride adorned for her husband" (Rev 21:2). A few verses later, the author declares Jerusalem to be "the bride, the wife of the Lamb" (Rev 21:9). Thus, in Revelation, both God and Jesus, the Lamb, share the status of bridegroom. Jerusalem, which contains all God's faithful people and Jesus' faithful followers, is the bride.

Naming Jesus Bridegroom employs the metaphor of wedding. God or Jesus is the bridegroom, and God's people and Jesus' followers are the bride. While some are prepared for the bridegroom's arrival, others have run out of oil. The feast, a very important part of the wedding, represents the union of God and Jesus and people. Those who remain faithful enter the banquet hall where they dine with the Creator of all and his Son, Jesus Christ, the Lamb.

Journal/Meditation: What other implications of the wedding metaphor might be applied to Jesus? to God? to people?

Prayer: Bridegroom, John the Baptist was your friend, who rejoiced greatly when you came into the world. He decreased while you increased. Help me to be prepared for your return so that I may enter the wedding feast with you and rejoice forever. You live and reign in eternal Trinity—Father, Son, and Holy Spirit—now and forever and ever. Amen.

True Vine

Scripture: Jesus said: "I am the true vine, and my Father is the vinegrower. He removes every branch in me that bears no fruit. Every branch that bears fruit he prunes to make it bear more fruit." (John 15:1–2)

Reflection: Throughout the Hebrew Bible (Old Testament), Israel is portrayed as a vine (Ps 80:8–16; Isa 5:1–7, 27:2–6; Jer 2:21). In John's Gospel Jesus names himself the true vine, God's vine, of life that flows into the branches: "Just as the branch cannot bear fruit by itself unless it abides in the vine, neither can [the disciples] unless [they] abide in [him]" (John 15:4b). Repeating himself and again using the divine name I AM, the Johannine Jesus states, "I am the vine, you are the branches" (John 15:5a). Thus, just like a grapevine supplies nourishment to the branches that grow on it, so Jesus is the source of eternal life for people who believe in him as long as they abide in him (John 15:5b).

"... [T]he branch cannot bear fruit by itself unless it abides in the vine" (John 15:4). Thus, neither can disciples unless they abide in Jesus. Whoever does not abide is pruned and thrown away. What the Johannine Jesus is speaking about—using the word *abide*—is the closeness that must exist between him and his followers. That closeness is modeled on the closeness that exists between Jesus and God. In other words, authentic Christian life is recognizing the unity that exists among all believers and doing everything to foster it. In the genuine Pauline letters, the apostle refers to this concept as the body of Christ; all the members form one body who are united, dependent, and subject to each other. The Johannine Jesus' image of vine and branches attempts to capture the same idea using a different metaphor.

In a world that fosters extreme individuality at the expense of the common good, the vine and branches metaphor (along with the body of Christ metaphor) serves as an antidote. Throughout biblical literature, the common good comes before the individual's good. What may be good for the individual has to be evaluated in terms of how it will affect the community. If it affects the common good in any negative way, the individual must submit himself or herself to what is good for all. The common good trumps the individual's good. Naming Jesus the True Vine means that a person understands this concept and lives it in his or her daily life.

Journal/Meditation: As a branch on the vine of Jesus Christ, in what specific ways do you put the common good ahead of your own good?

Prayer: True Vine, your Father is the vinegrower who removes every branch in you that bears no fruit and who prunes those who do so they bear more fruit. Keep me ever attached to you that I may share your life now and enjoy it for all eternity. You are one God with the Father and the Holy Spirit forever and ever. Amen.

Emmanuel

Scripture: "All this took place to fulfill what had been spoken by the Lord through the prophet: 'Look, the virgin shall conceive and bear a son, and they shall name him Emmanuel,' which means, 'God is with us.'" (Matt 1:22–23)

Reflection: Because the author of Matthew's Gospel desires to present Jesus as the fulfillment of one predicted and hoped for by the prophets, he loves to quote Hebrew Bible (Old Testament) material out of context. Such is the case of the quotation presented above. Either the author of Matthew's Gospel did not know from which prophet came the words he was using or he preferred not to identify his source; the phrase comes from Isaiah in a totally different context. The prophet attempts to offer hope to King Ahaz, who was embroiled in politics. According to Isaiah, the Davidic lineage will not be extinguished because "the young woman is with child and shall bear a son, and shall name him Immanuel" (Isa 7:14).

Two important points need to be explored. First, the young woman is probably one of King Ahaz's wives, who will give birth to a prince who will sit on Judah's throne. The birth of a son in a monarchical system insures the future. Second, it was not uncommon to give names to people in order to indicate their function. Isaiah has previously presented children whose names reveal something God is doing. For example, Isaiah's son, Shear-ja-shub, is presented to Ahaz; the name means a remnant shall return (Isa 7:3). The name Emmanuel (or Immanuel) given to Ahaz's son indicates that God is with the Davidic monarch, and that the monarchy will not disappear. In its historical context, the quotation means something different from what the author of Matthew's Gospel determines it to mean.

In fact, the First Gospel's meaning is not discovered until the end of the book. The resurrected and appearing Matthean Jesus' last line to his disciples is this: "I am with you always, to the end of the age" (Matt 28:20b). While the author of Luke's Gospel presents an ascension, a disappearance of the risen Jesus, the author of Matthew's Gospel presents the meaning of Emmanuel: God, in the person of Jesus, is with us. Thus, the gospel's bookends proclaim the presence of God in Jesus Christ. To name Jesus Emmanuel is to declare that God is with people.

Journal/Meditation: In what specific ways do you recognize the presence of God with you? What are the signs or other names for his presence?

Prayer: Emmanuel, the prophet Isaiah proclaimed the LORD's presence with the Israelites of old. The author of Matthew's Gospel proclaimed you to be the new presence of God with people. Make me more aware of the divine Trinitarian dwelling. You, Lord Jesus Christ, live and reign with the Father and the Holy Spirit, one God, forever and ever. Amen.

Amen

Scripture: "The words of the Amen, the faithful and true witness, the origin of God's creation: I know your works; you are neither cold nor hot. I wish that you were either cold or hot." (Rev 3:14b–15)

Reflection: In the Christian Bible (New Testament) the only place where Jesus is named Amen is in the Book of Revelation. The Hebrew word *amen* means firmness or certainty. It can also be translated as truly, yes, or it is true, as is indicated in the passage above. Jesus, the Amen, is the faithful and true witness; his word is worthy of trust. While Paul does not name Jesus Amen, he alludes to the same idea in his Second Letter to the Corinthians. He writes: ". . . [T]he Son of God, Jesus Christ, whom we proclaimed among you, . . . was not 'Yes and No'; but in him it is always 'Yes.' For in him every one of God's promises is a 'Yes.' For this reason it is through him that we say the 'Amen,' to the glory of God" (2 Cor 1:19–20). In other words, Jesus represents the final Yes, the final Amen, to God's work. As the passage above presents it, Jesus is the witness whose testimony never falls short of the truth.

The passage above is from one of seven letters addressed to seven different communities known to the pseudonymous author, John of Patmos. John is told to write to the church in Laodicea, explaining how the members of that community are neither cold nor hot, that is, they are neither Yes nor No. The risen Jesus dictates the letter to John, stating, "so, because you are lukewarm, and neither cold nor hot, I am about to spit you out of my mouth" (Rev 3:16). While the context is unknown to modern readers, the author of the passage knows that the water supply of Laodicea was warm. By the time the water from the hot springs of Hierapolis reached Laodicea, it had become lukewarm. In his application to the members of the church, the author tells the people that they are ineffective in contrast to the Amen.

In naming Jesus Amen, the faithful, the true, the Yes, a person desires to foster the same commitment to God's work as that given by Jesus. For example, it is easy to remain lukewarm when faced with others' poverty, but it takes heat to volunteer in a soup kitchen, food pantry, or another place that serves the poor. One can remain lukewarm inside on a snowy day, but it takes heat to bundle up, go outside, and shovel the neighbor's driveway. The value of honesty remains lukewarm as long as it has no consequences that require heat to keep it. Naming Jesus Amen means that our works are known to God as yes, hot, and true.

Journal/Meditation: What recent work have you done that demonstrates that you are Amen, yes, hot, and true? Explain.

Prayer: Amen, faithful and true witness, you know my works; you know when I am cold or hot or lukewarm. Send the warm breath of the Holy Spirit to be my guide. Pour on me the heated grace of your Father. And grant that I may serve you faithfully all the days of my life. You are one God—Father, Son, and Holy Spirit—now and forever and ever. Amen.

Recent Books by Mark G. Boyer

Nature Spirituality: Praying with Wind, Water, Earth, Fire

A Spirituality of Ageing

Caroling through Advent and Christmas: Daily Reflections with Familiar Hymns

Weekday Saints: Reflections on Their Scriptures

Human Wholeness: A Spirituality of Relationship

The Liturgical Environment: What the Documents Say (third edition)

A Simple Systematic Mariology

Praying Your Way through Luke's Gospel and the Acts of the Apostles

Daybreaks: Daily Reflections for Advent and Christmas

Daybreaks: Daily Reflections for Lent and Easter

An Abecedarian of Animal Spirit Guides: Spiritual Growth through Reflections on Creatures

Overcome with Paschal Joy: Chanting through Lent and Easter —Daily Reflections with Familiar Hymns

Taking Leave of Your Home: Moving in the Peace of Christ

A Spirituality of Mission: Reflections for Holy Week and Easter

An Abecedarian of Sacred Trees: Spiritual Growth through Reflections on Woody Plants

Divine Presence: Elements of Biblical Theophanies

Fruit of the Vine: A Biblical Spirituality of Wine